I0135638

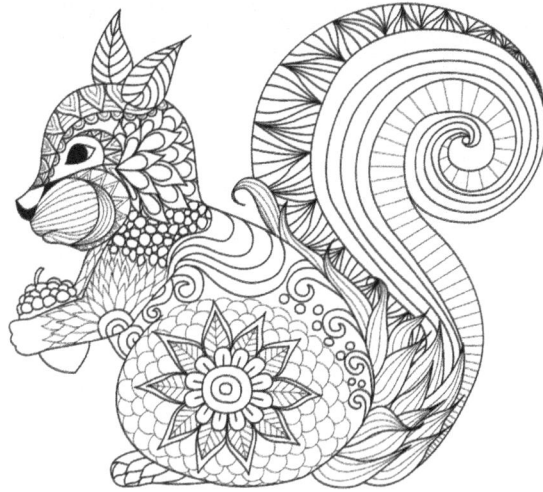

Forest Animals

Coloring Book

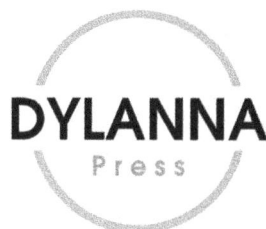

DYLANNA
Press

Copyright © 2020 by Dylanna Press

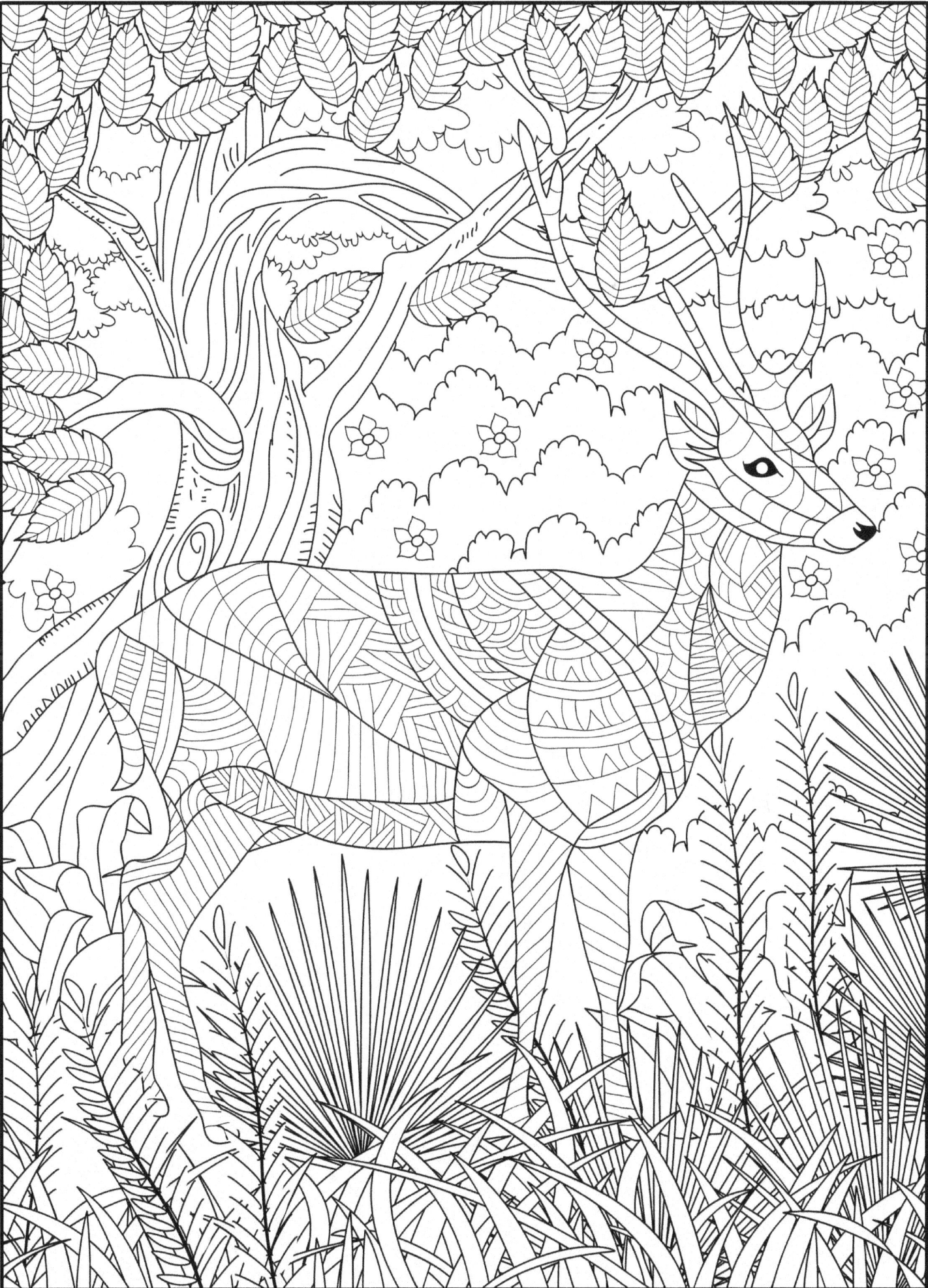

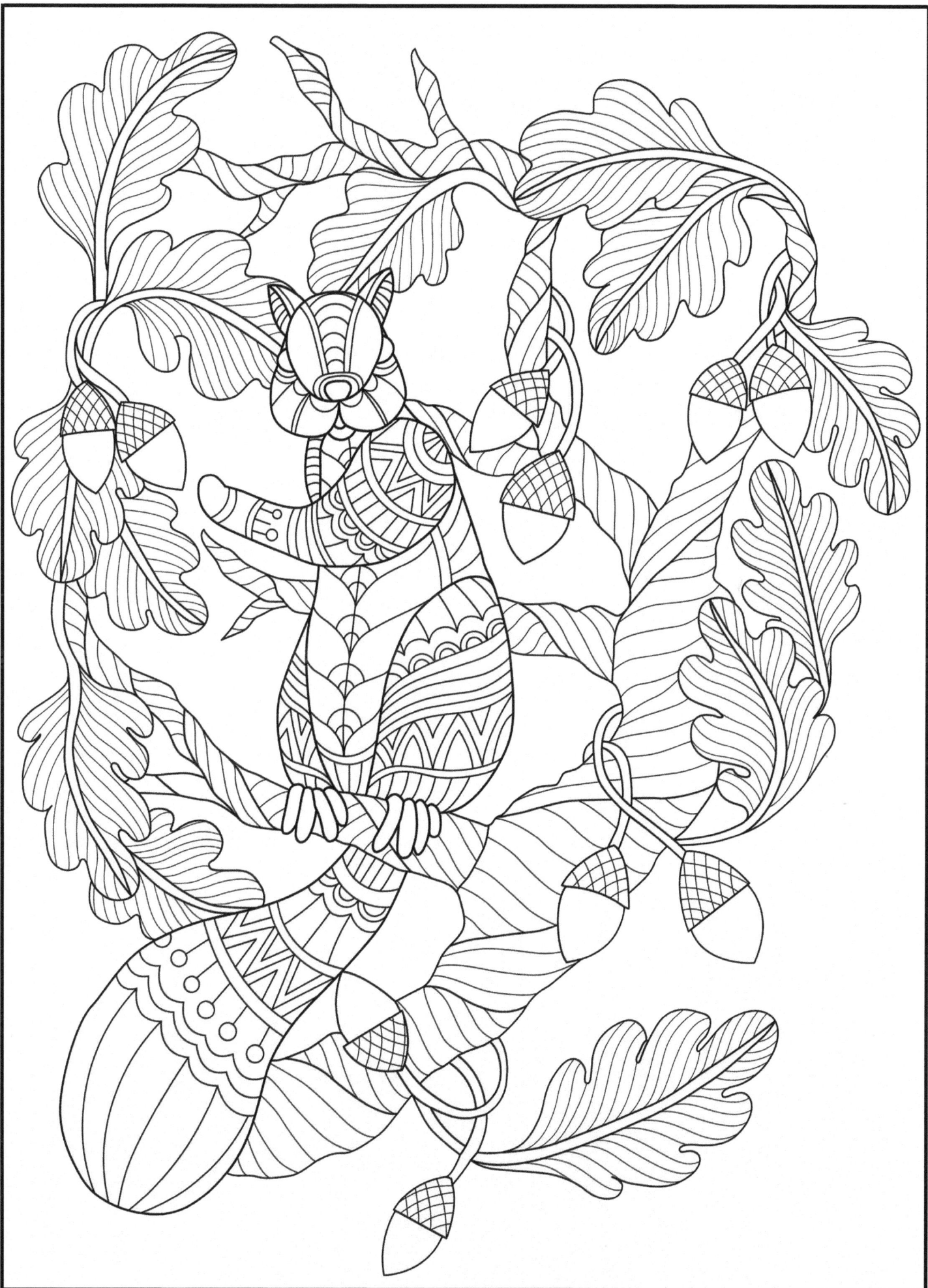

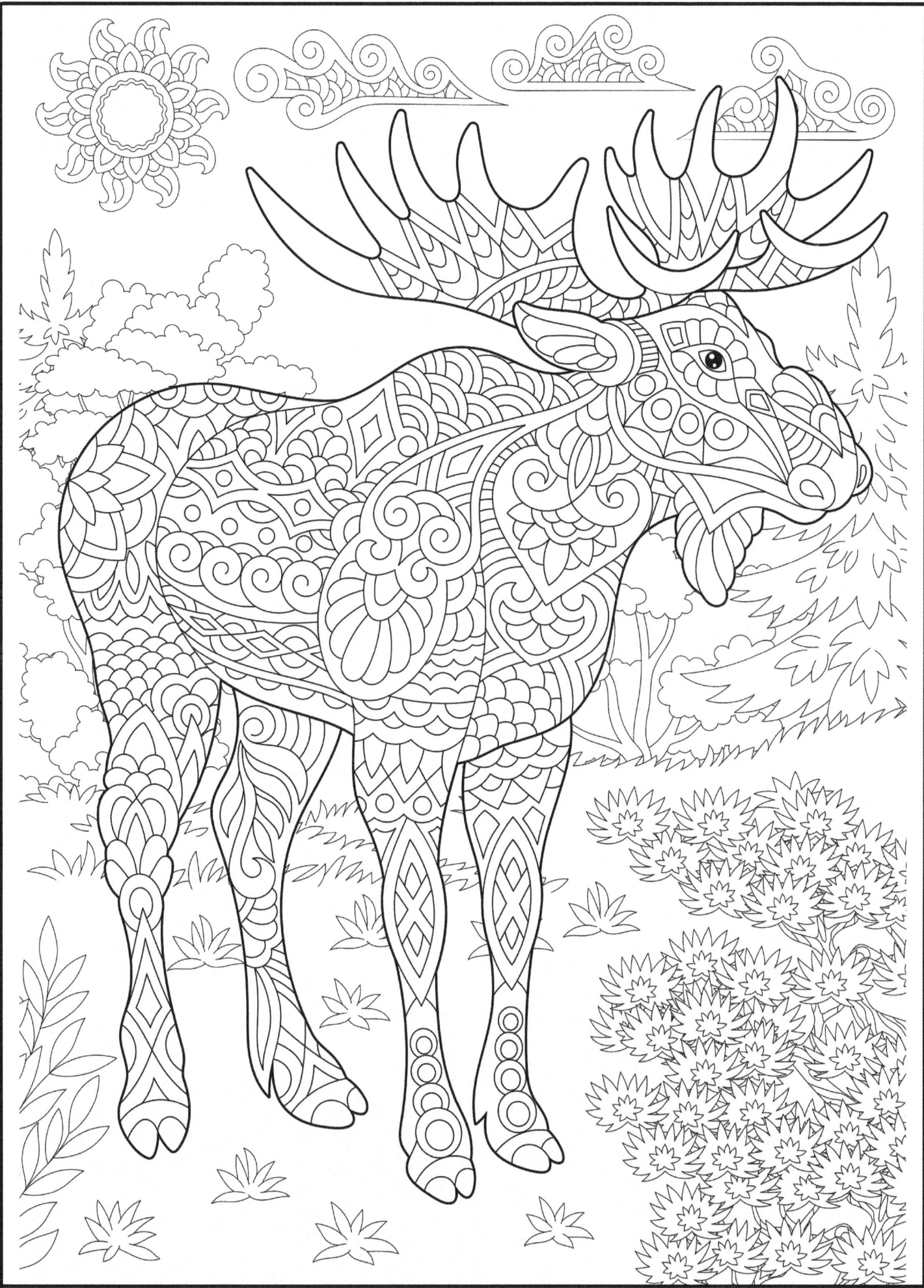

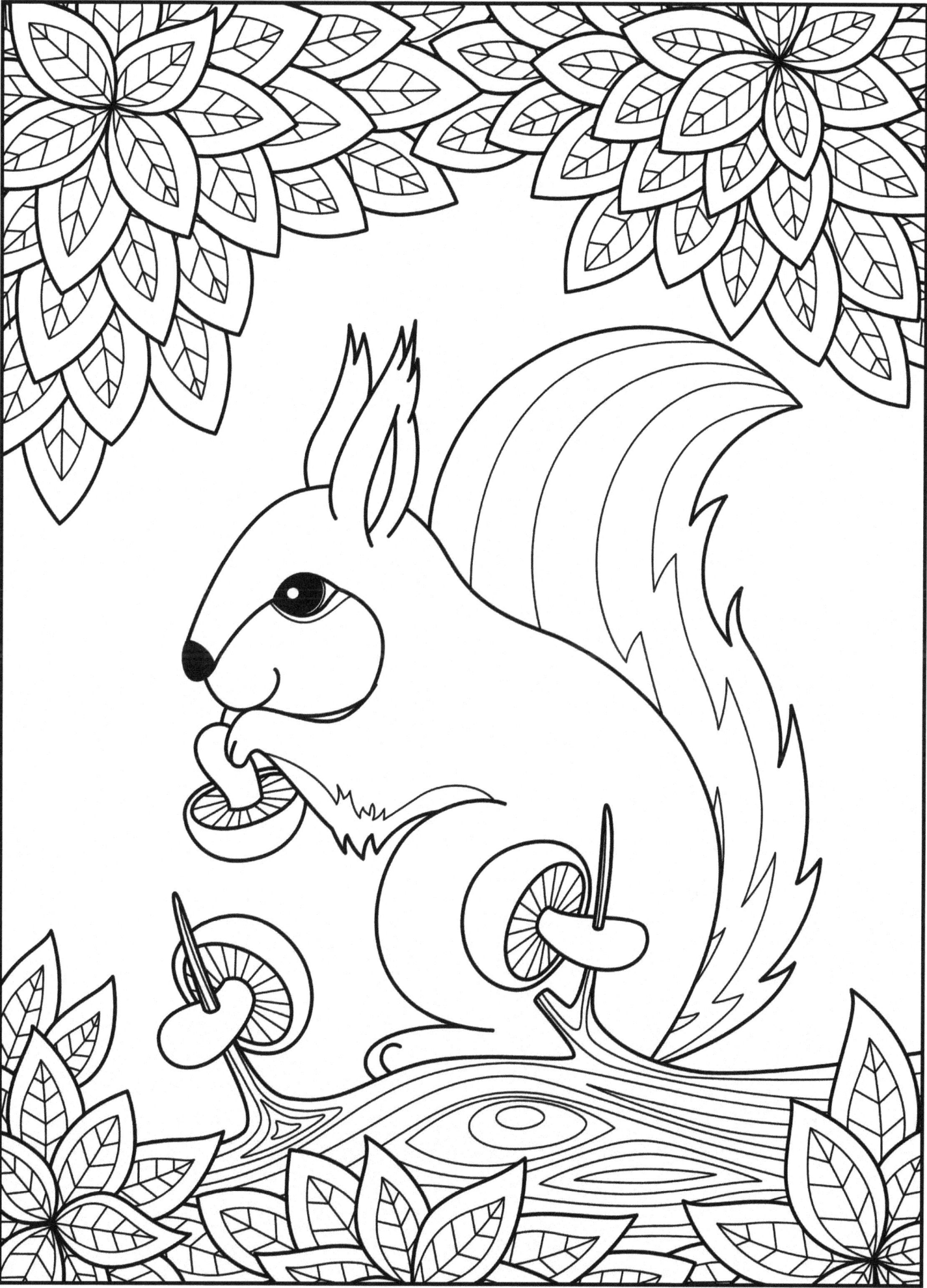

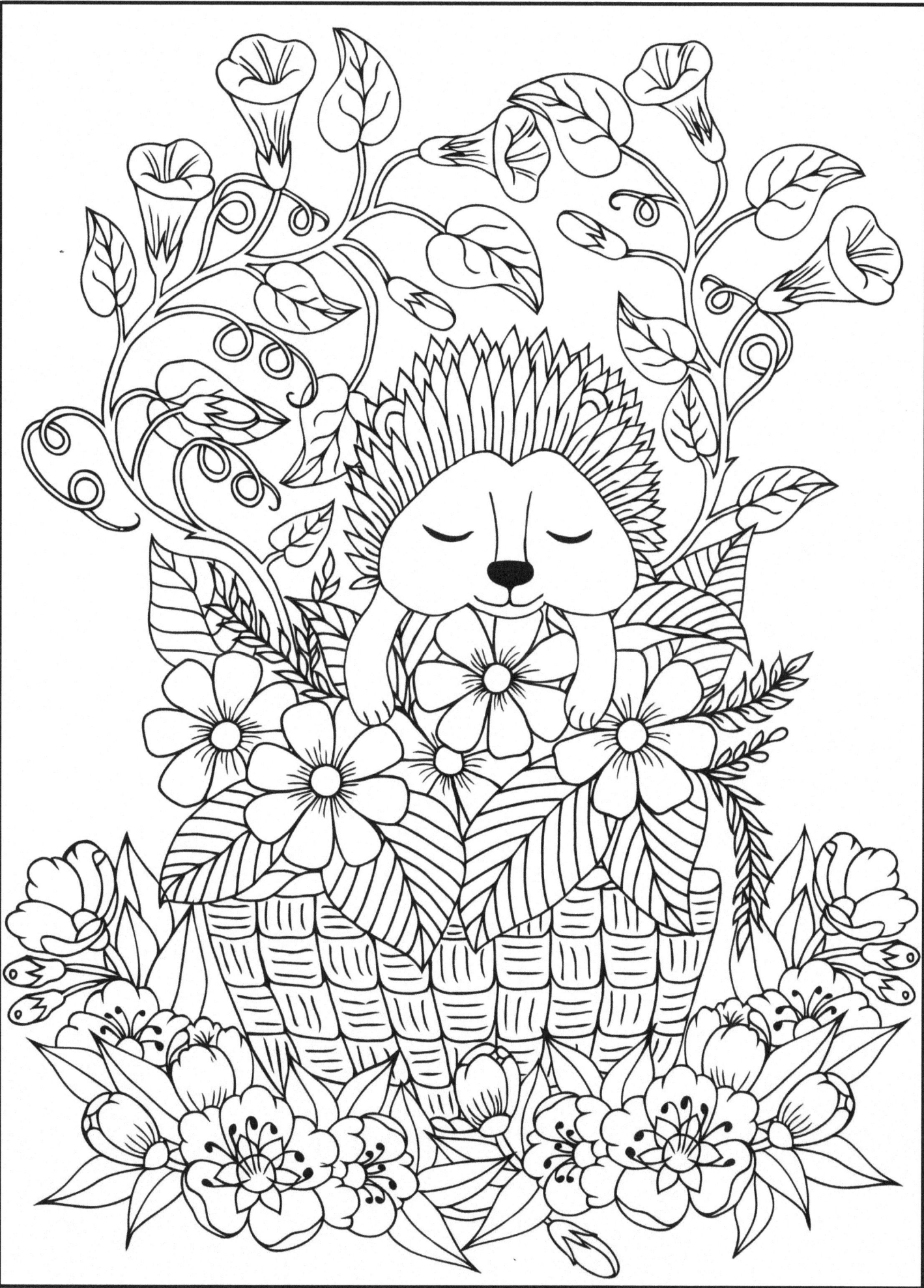

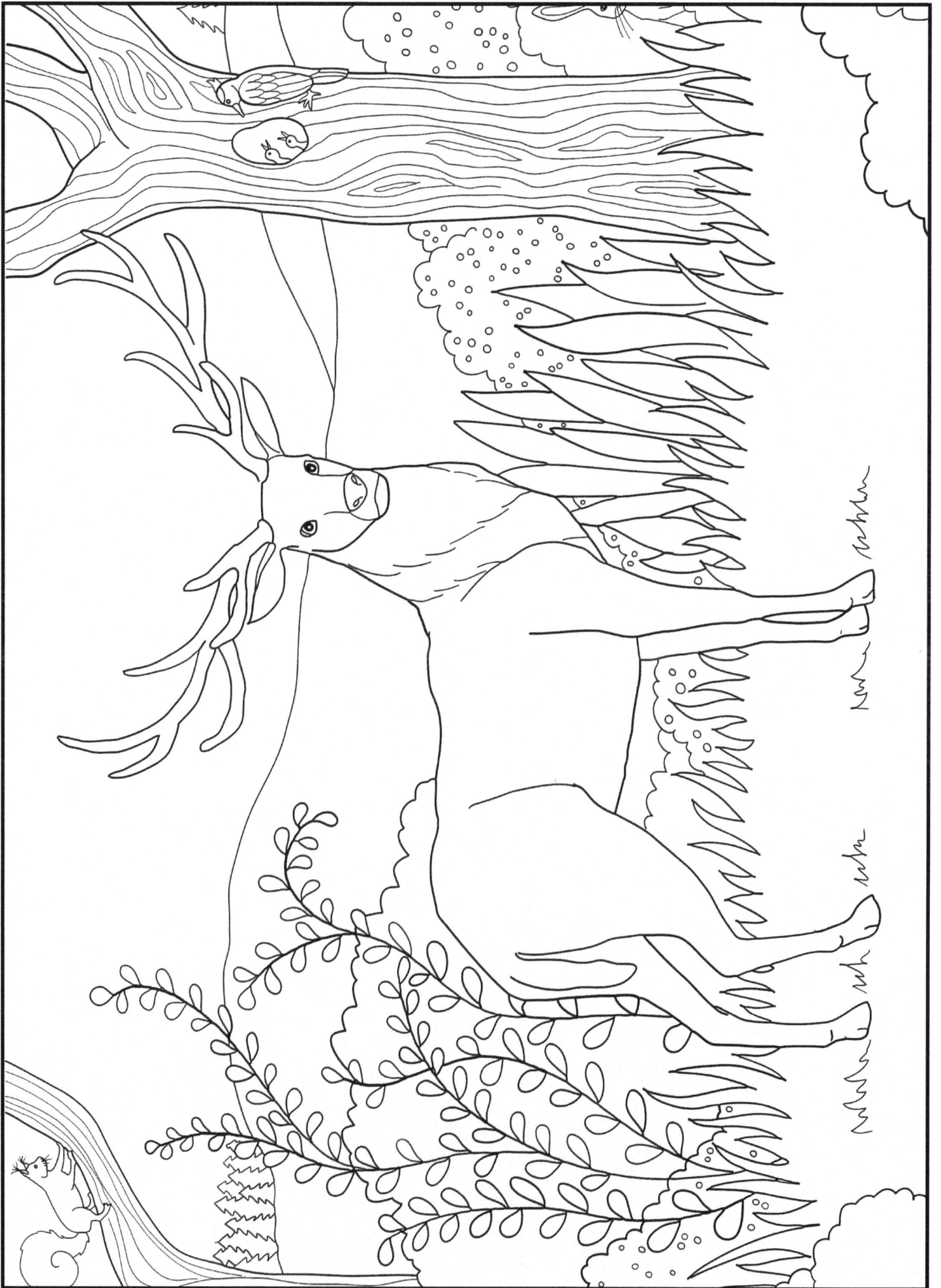

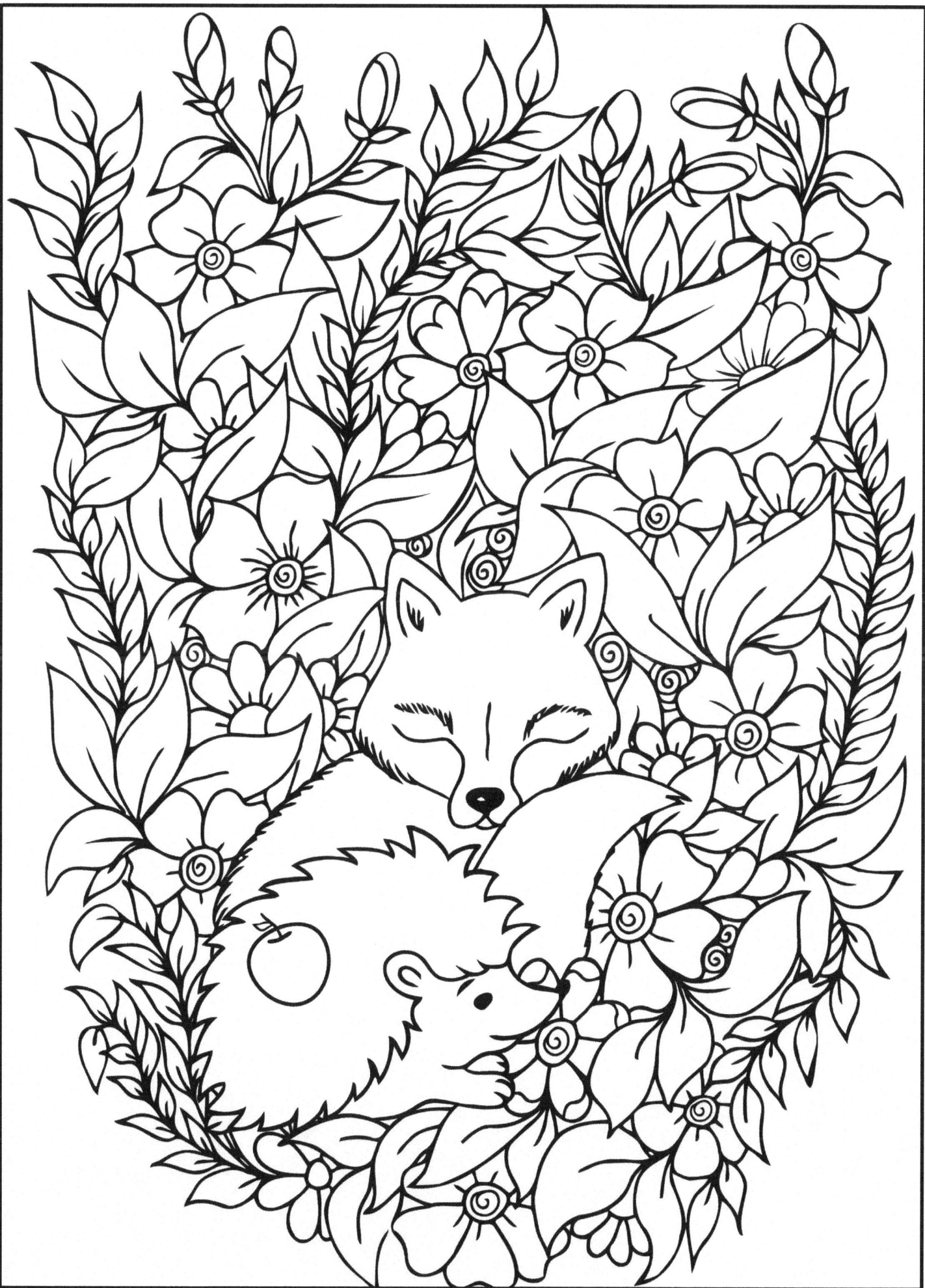

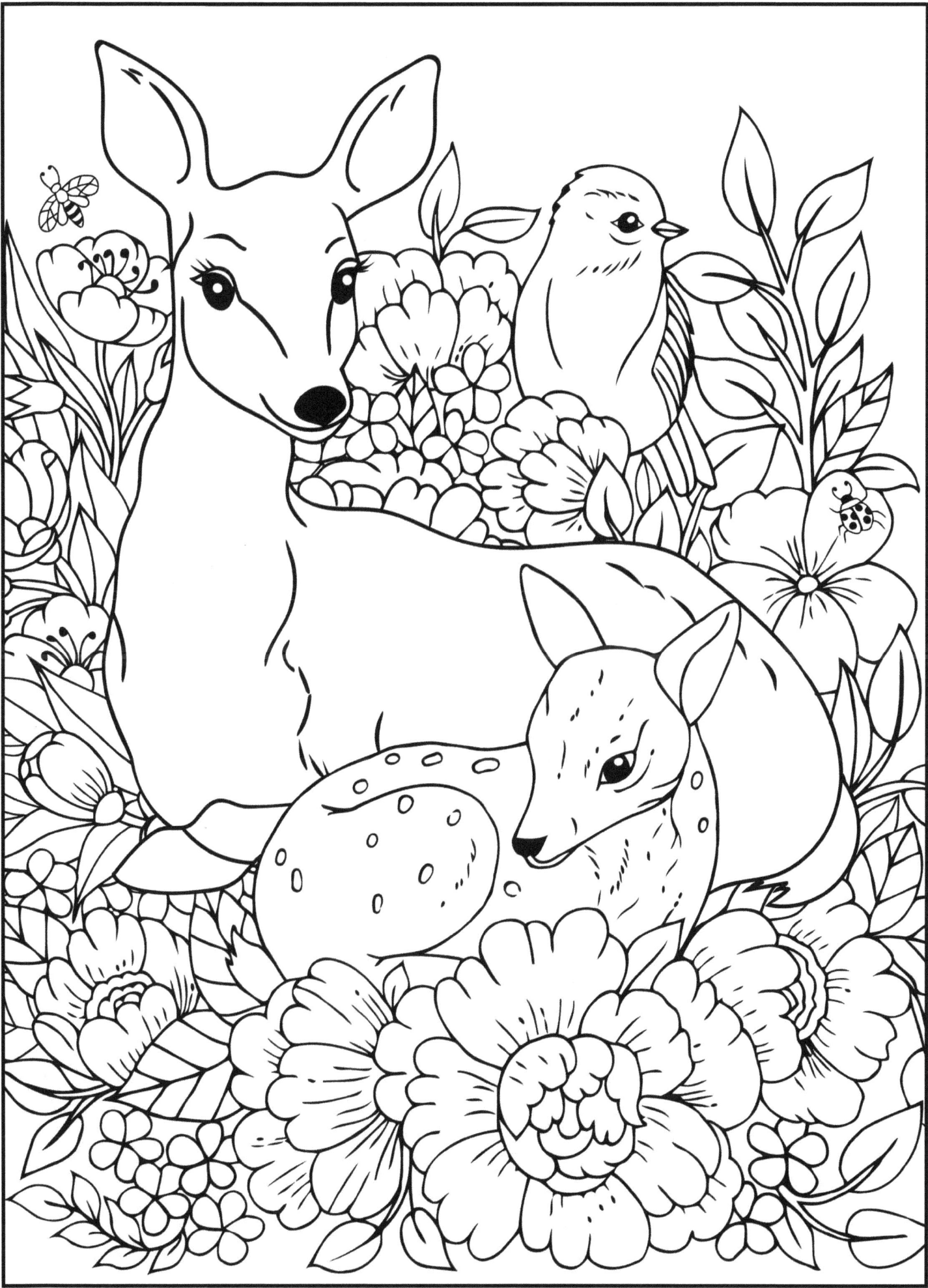

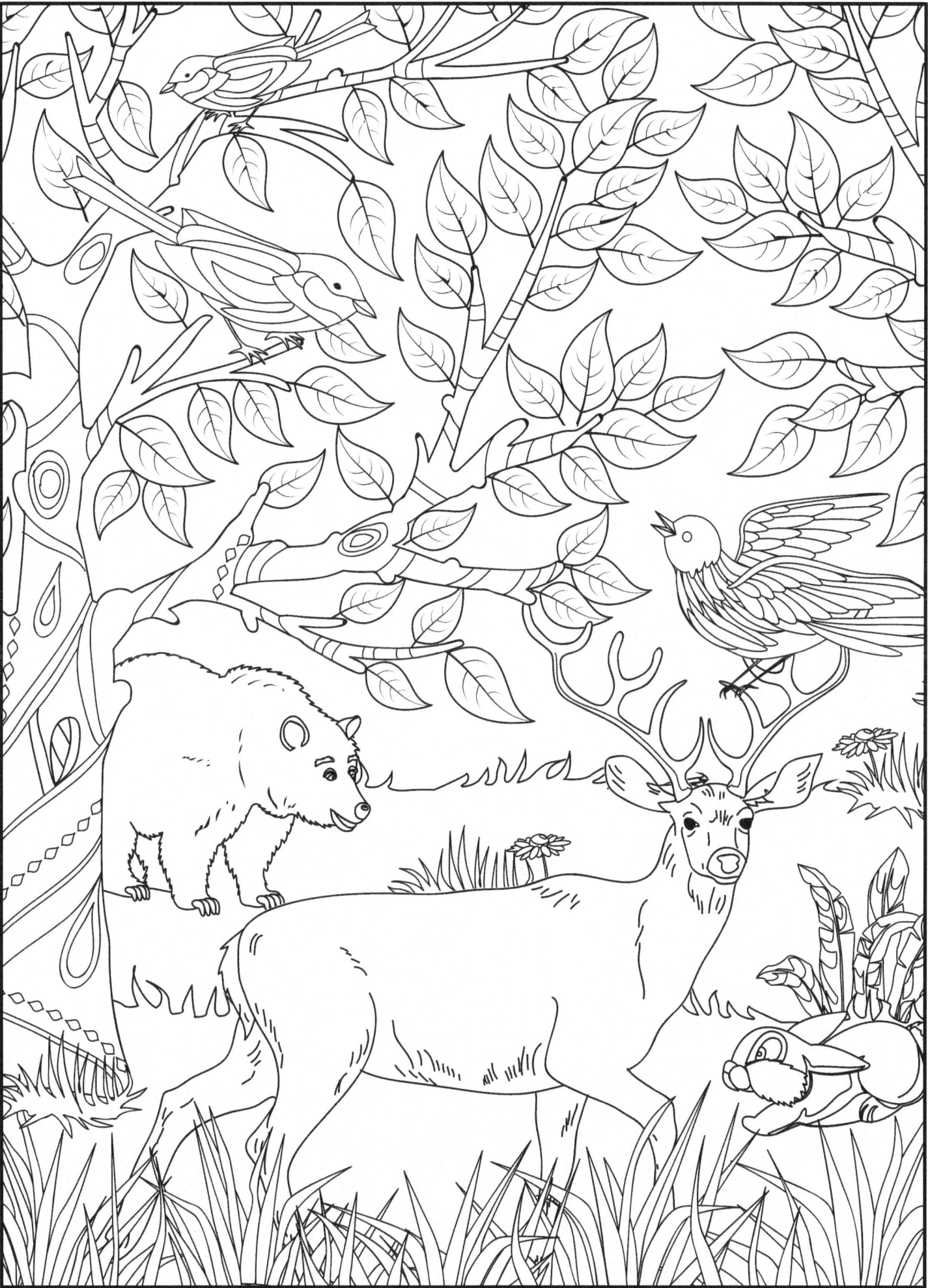

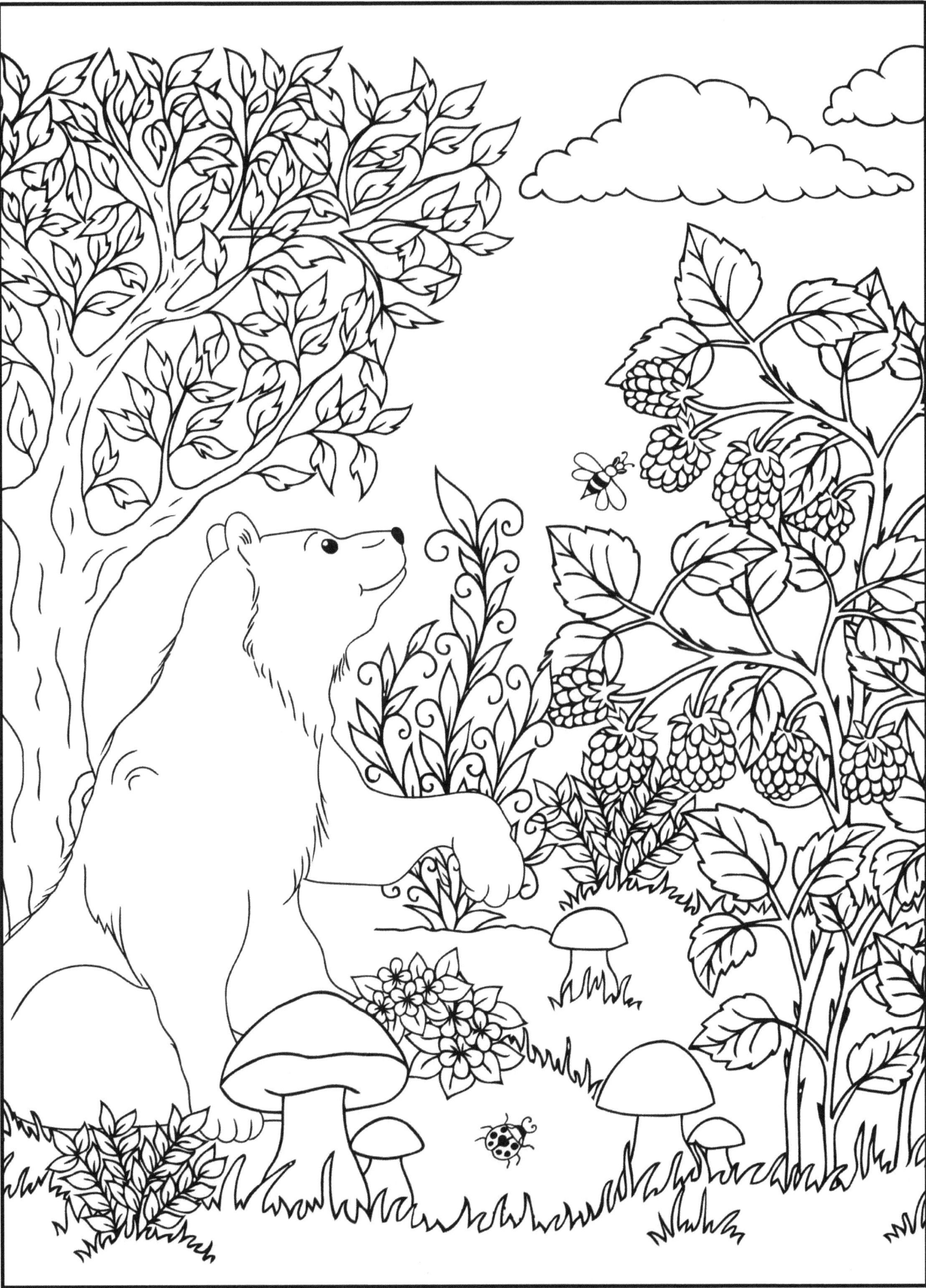

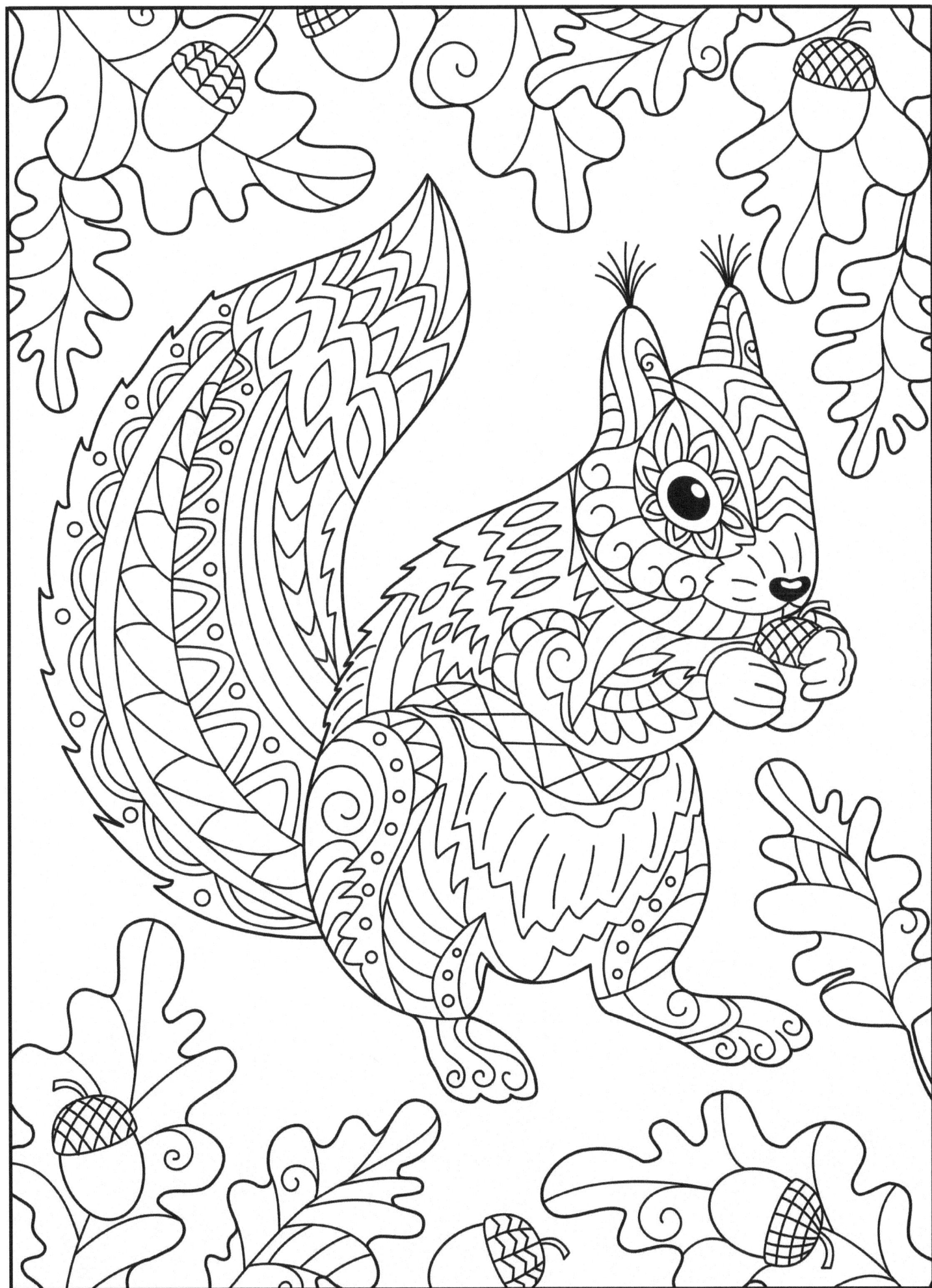

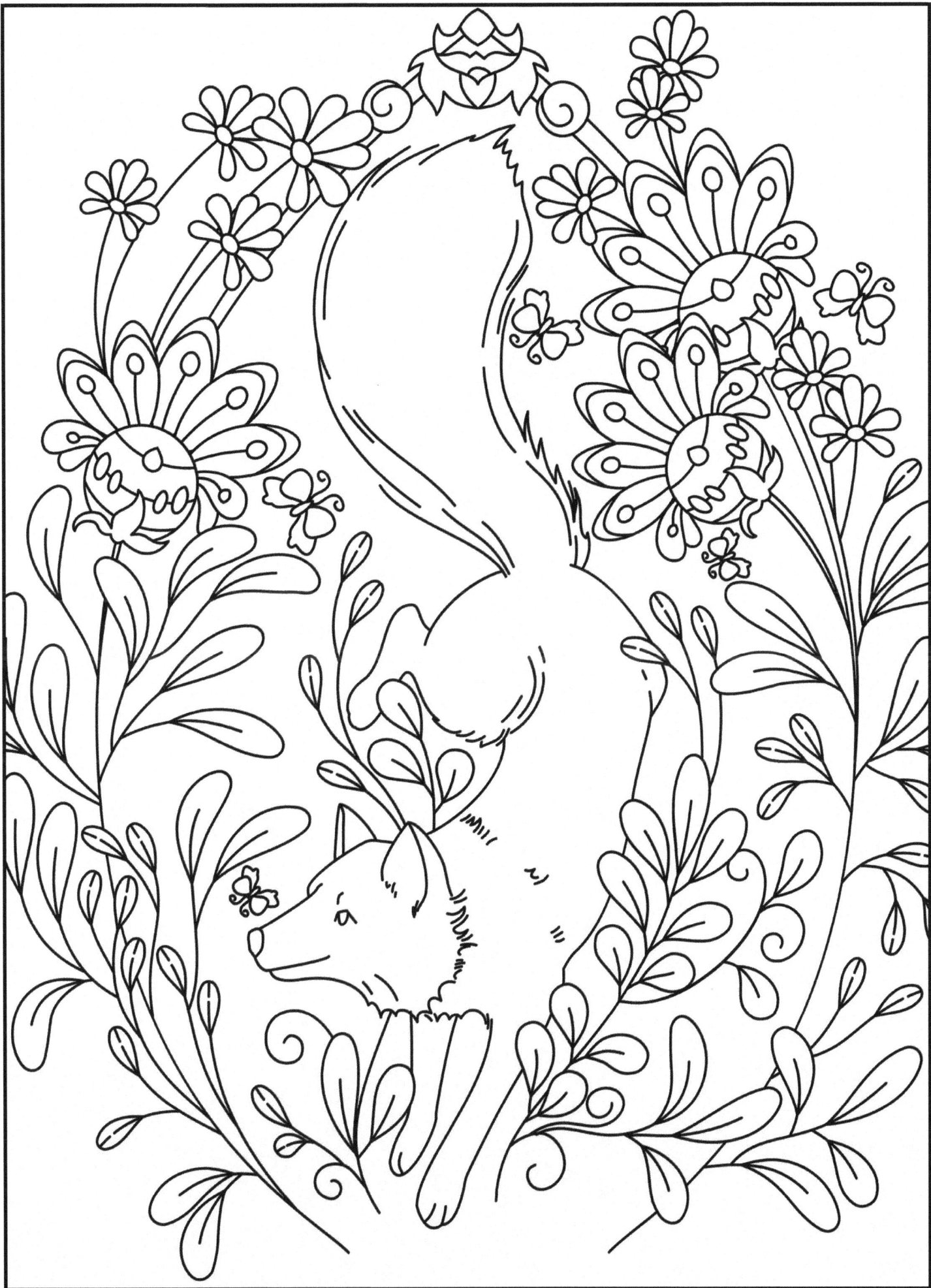

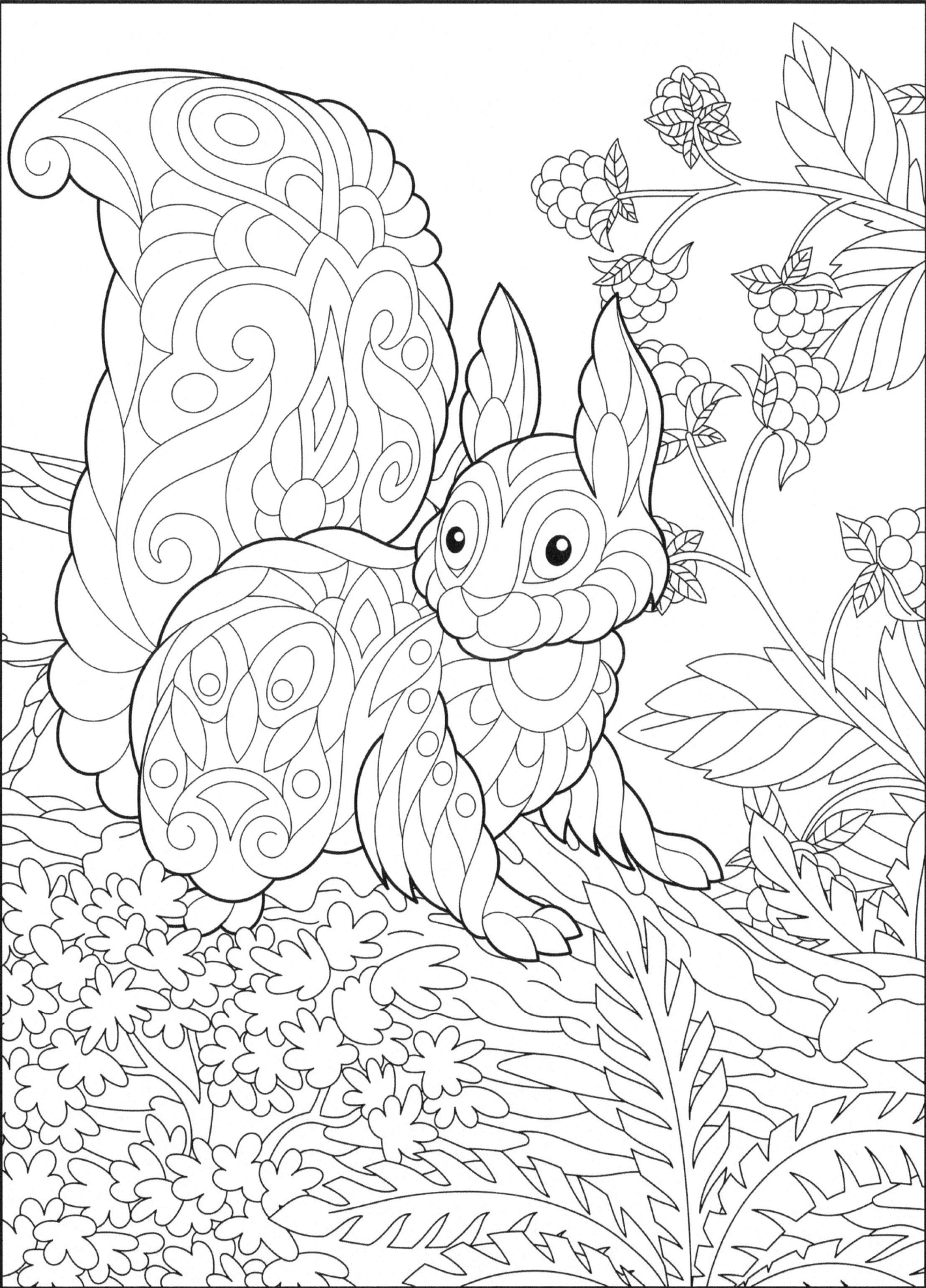

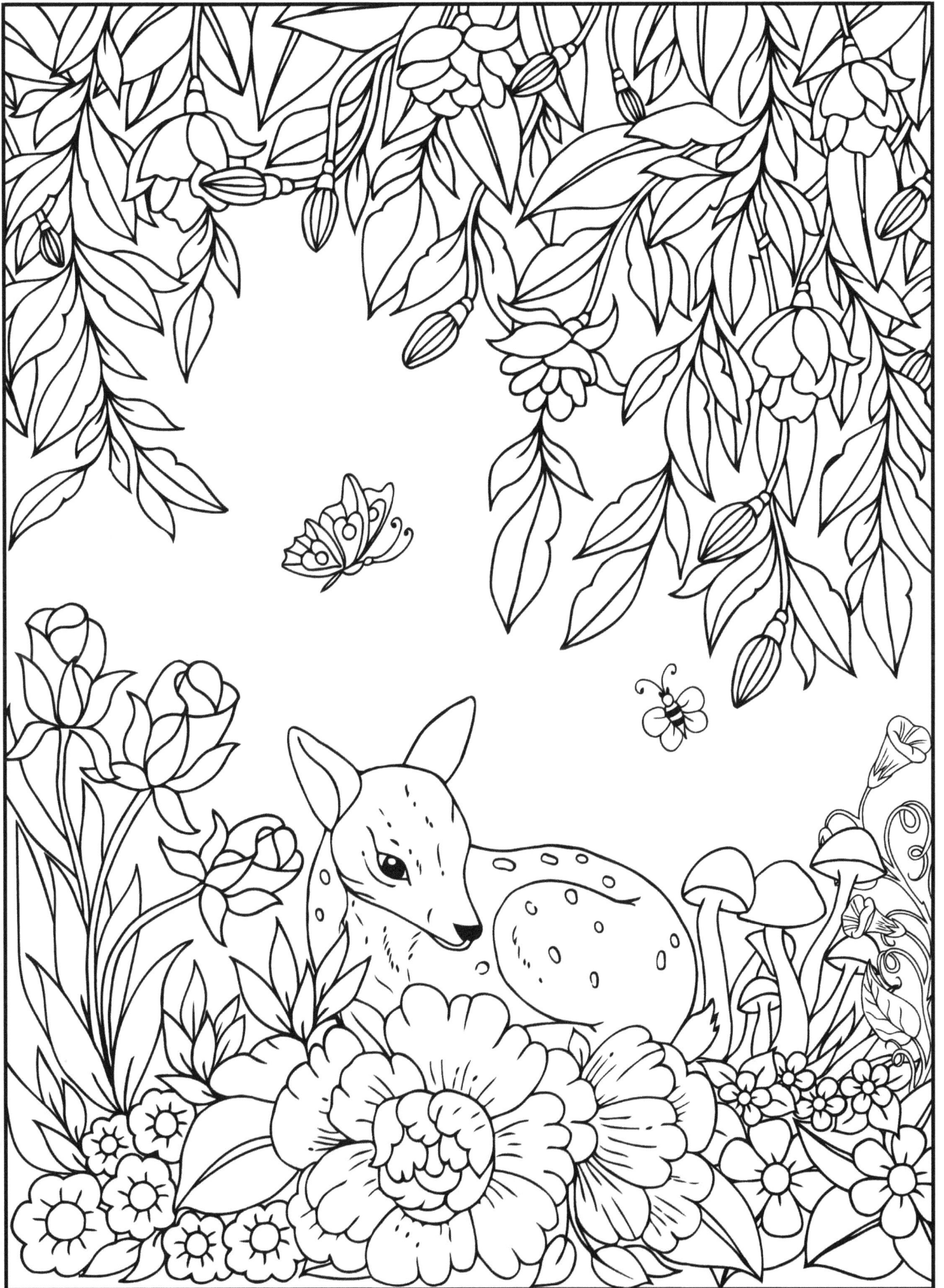

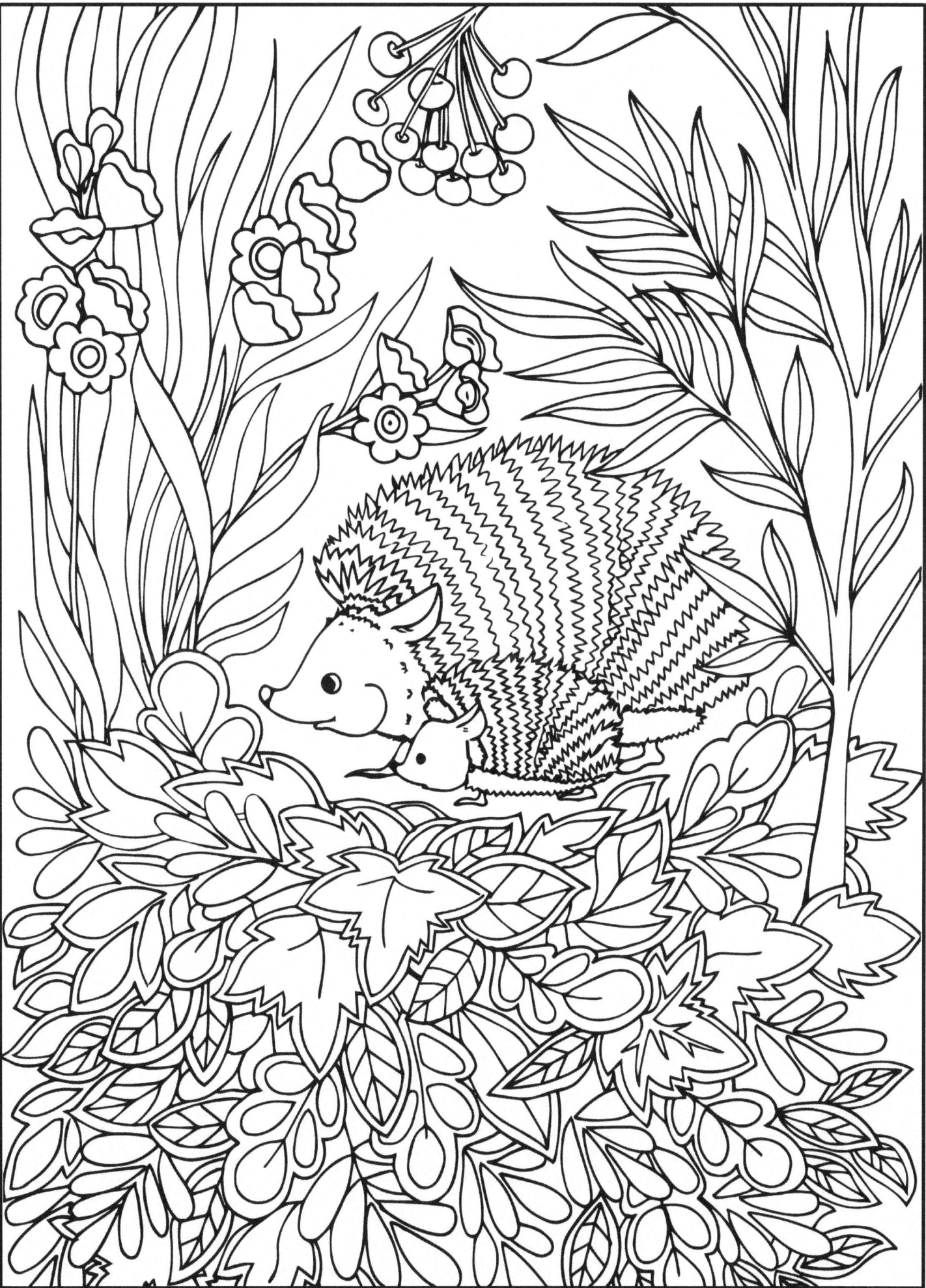

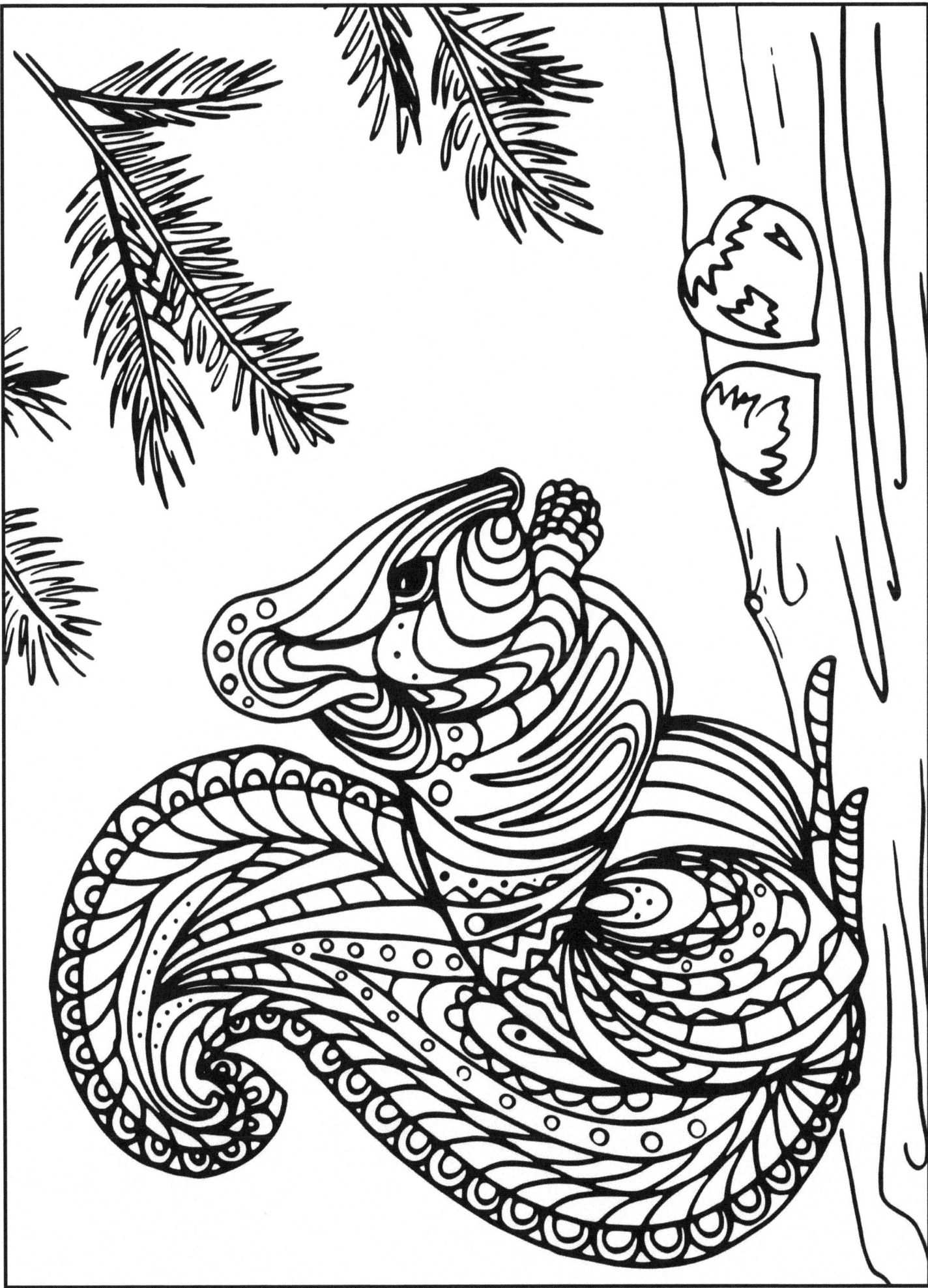

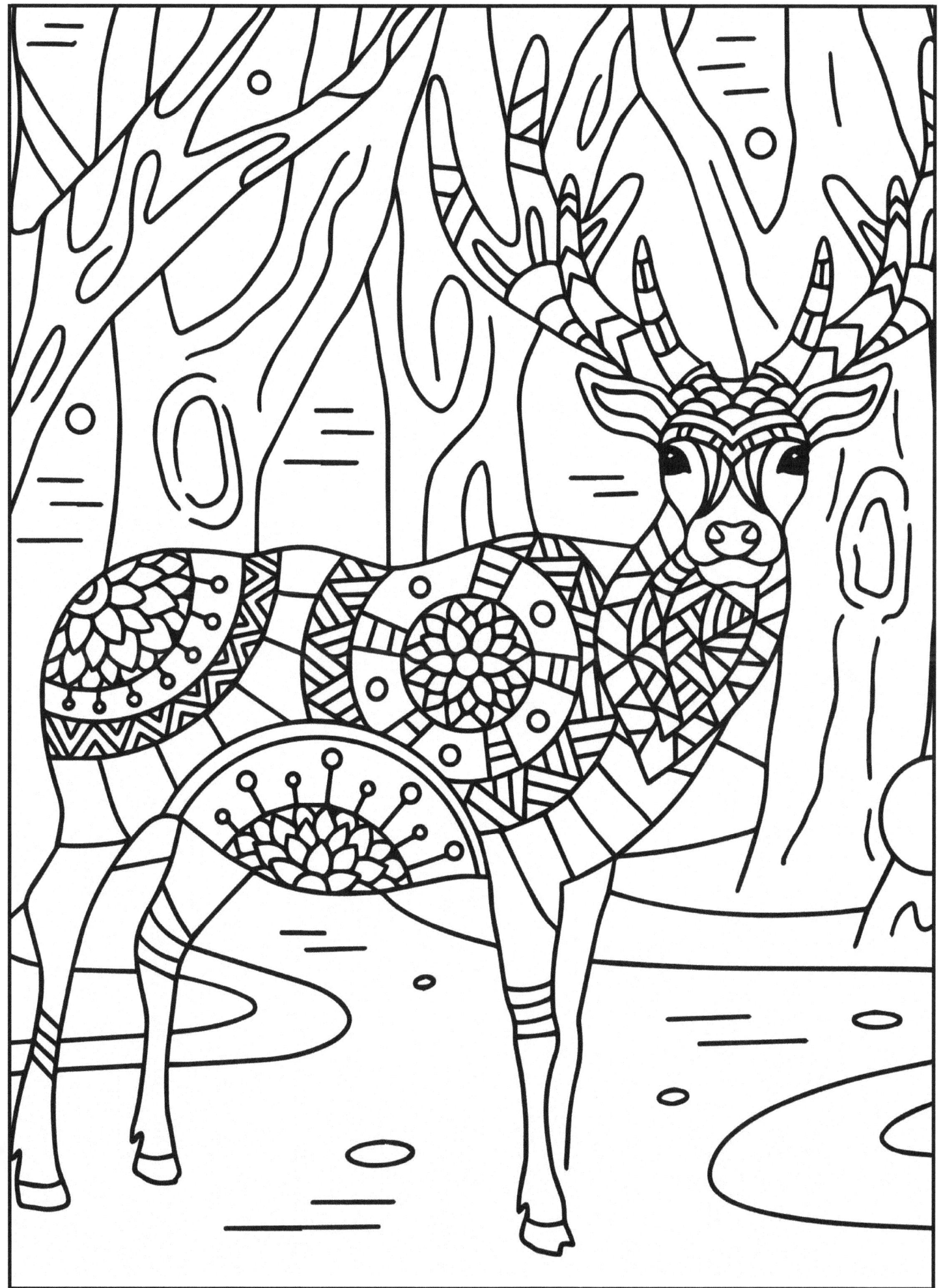

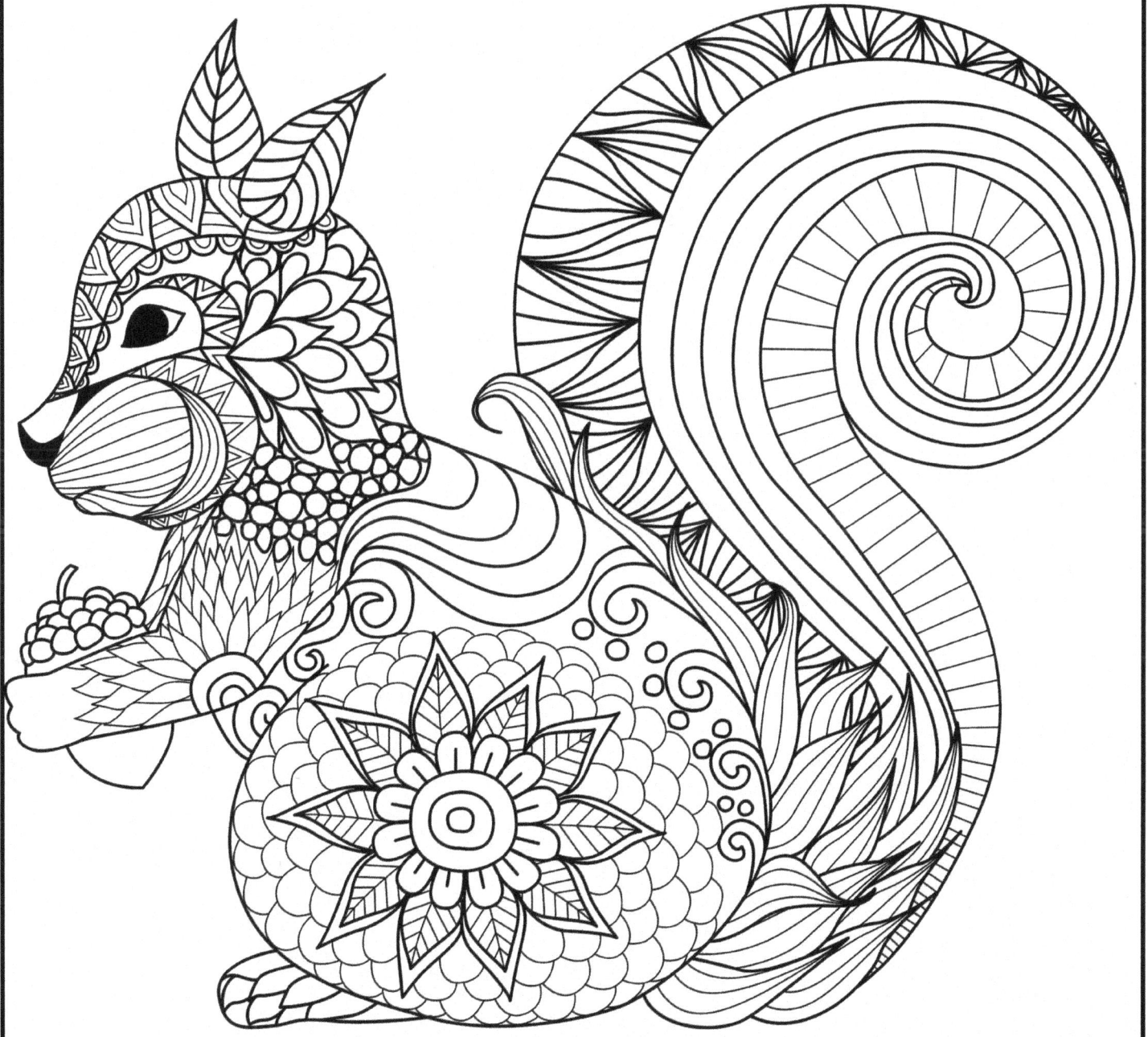

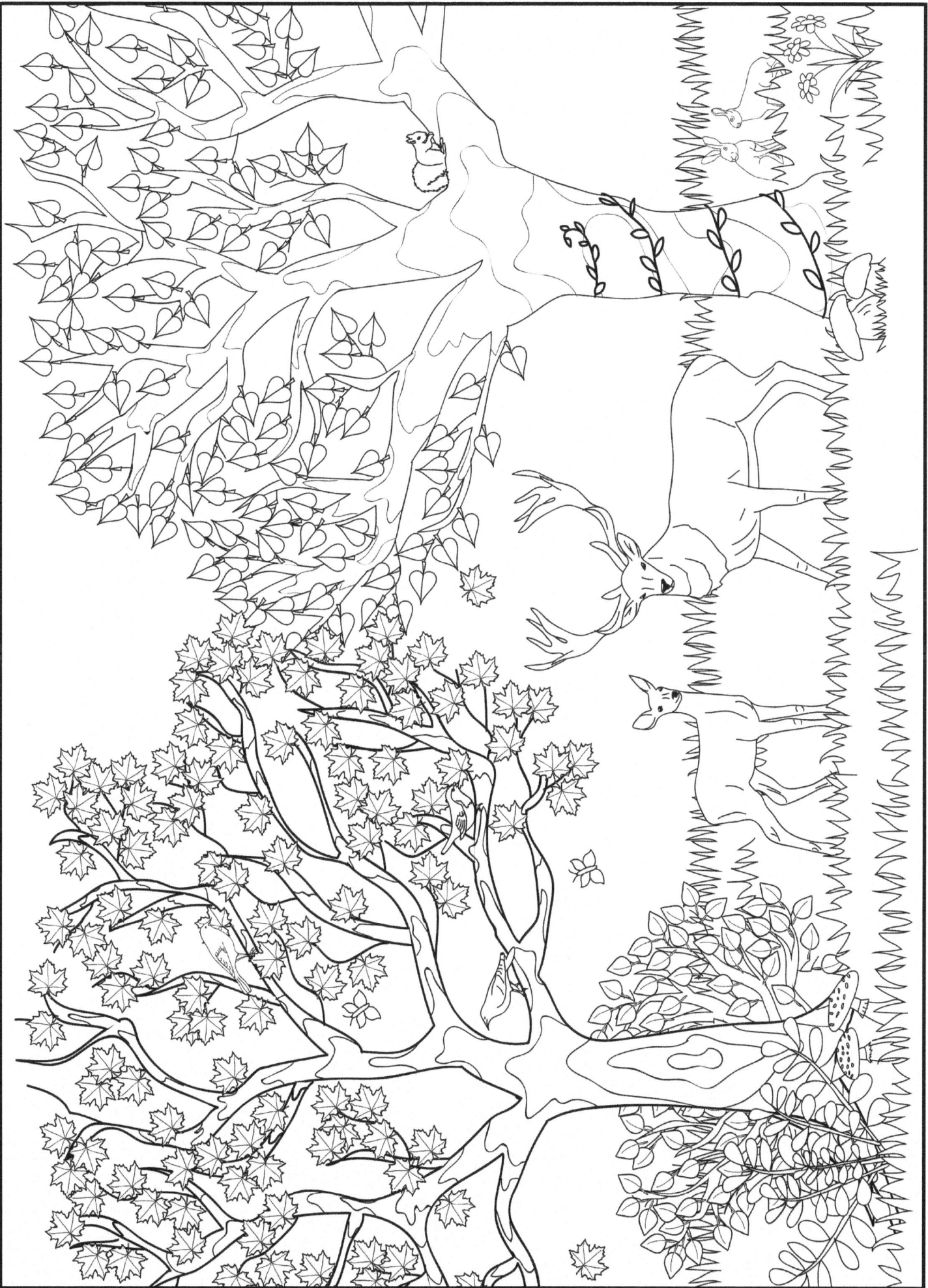

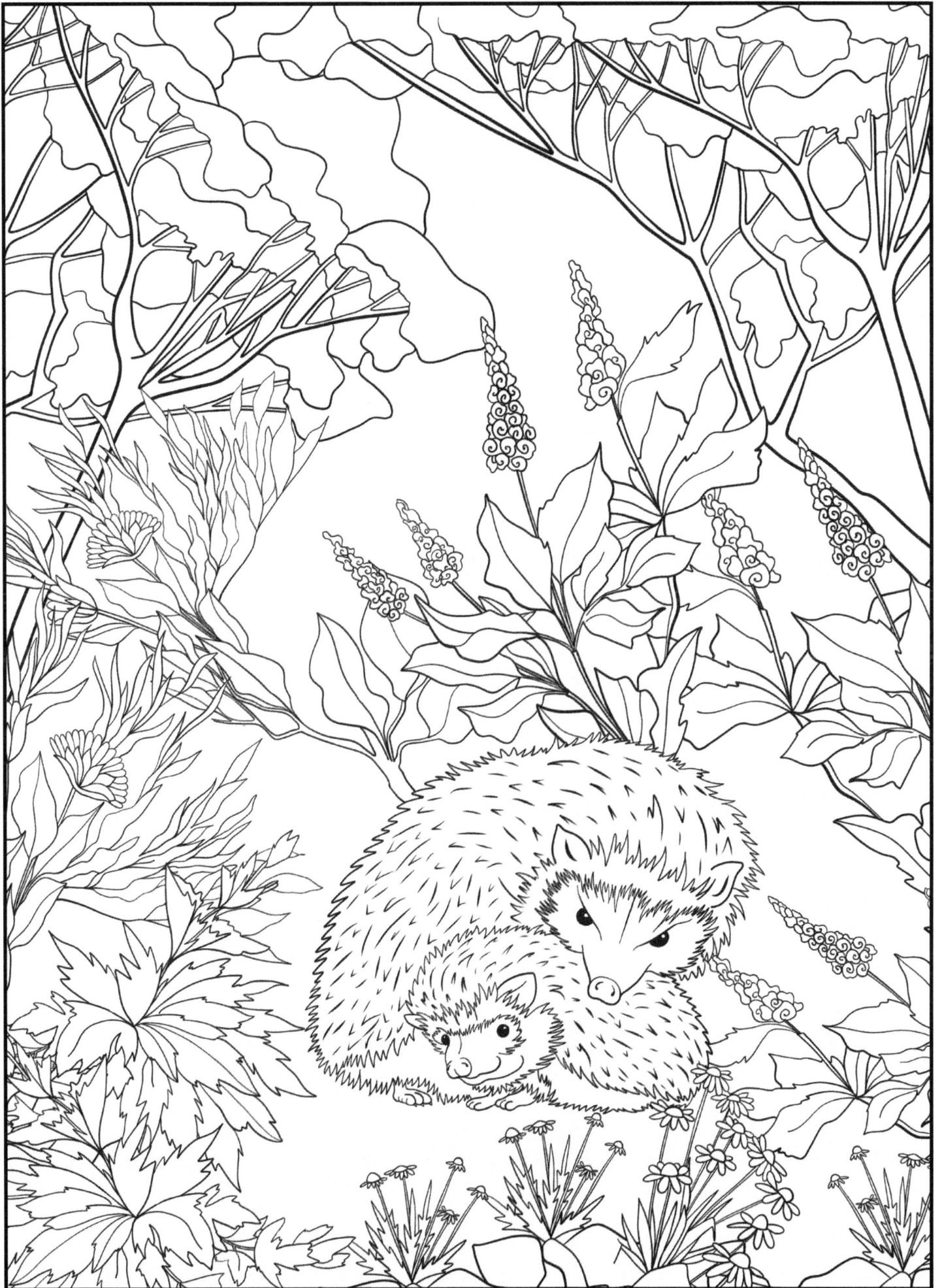

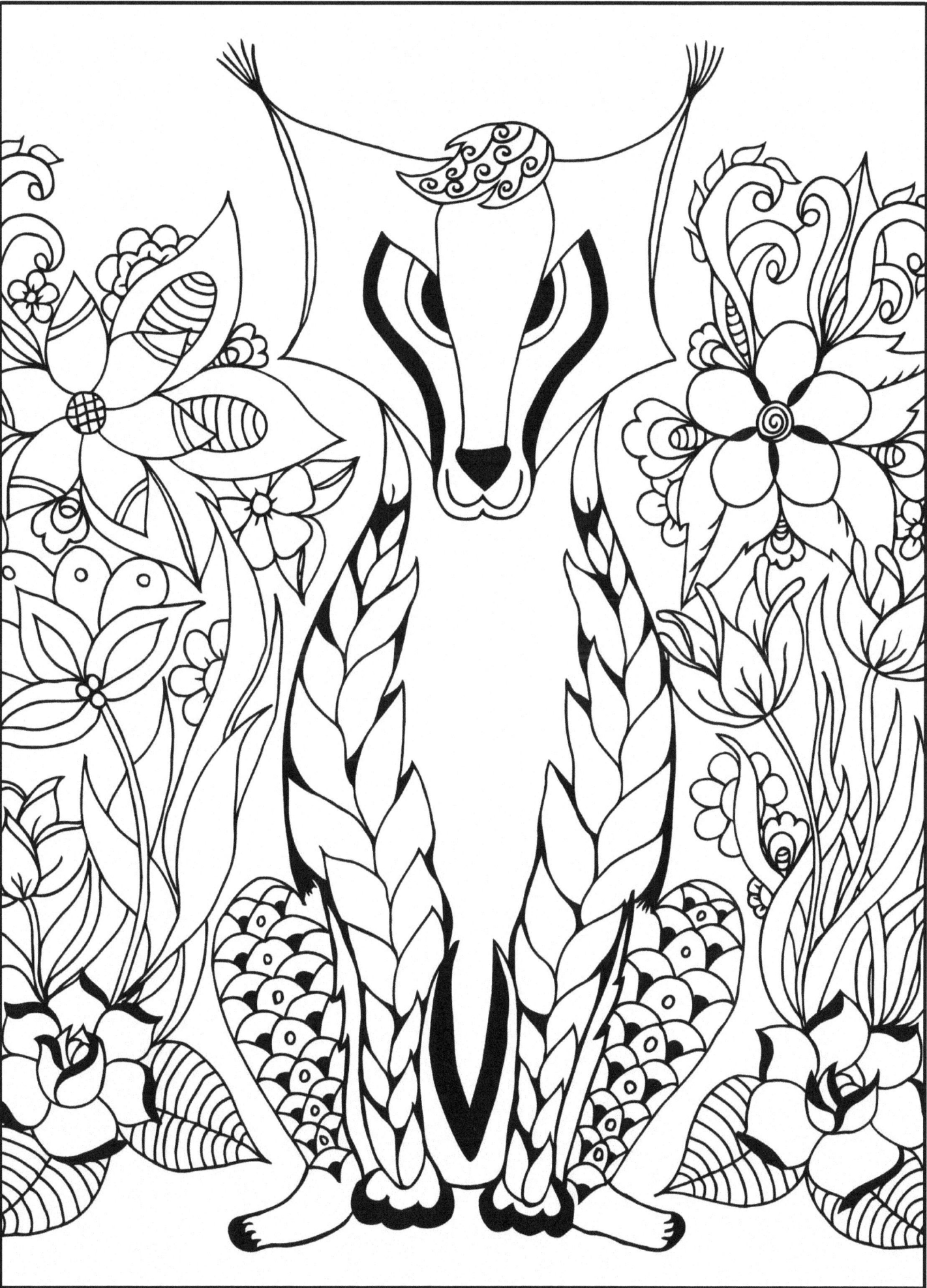

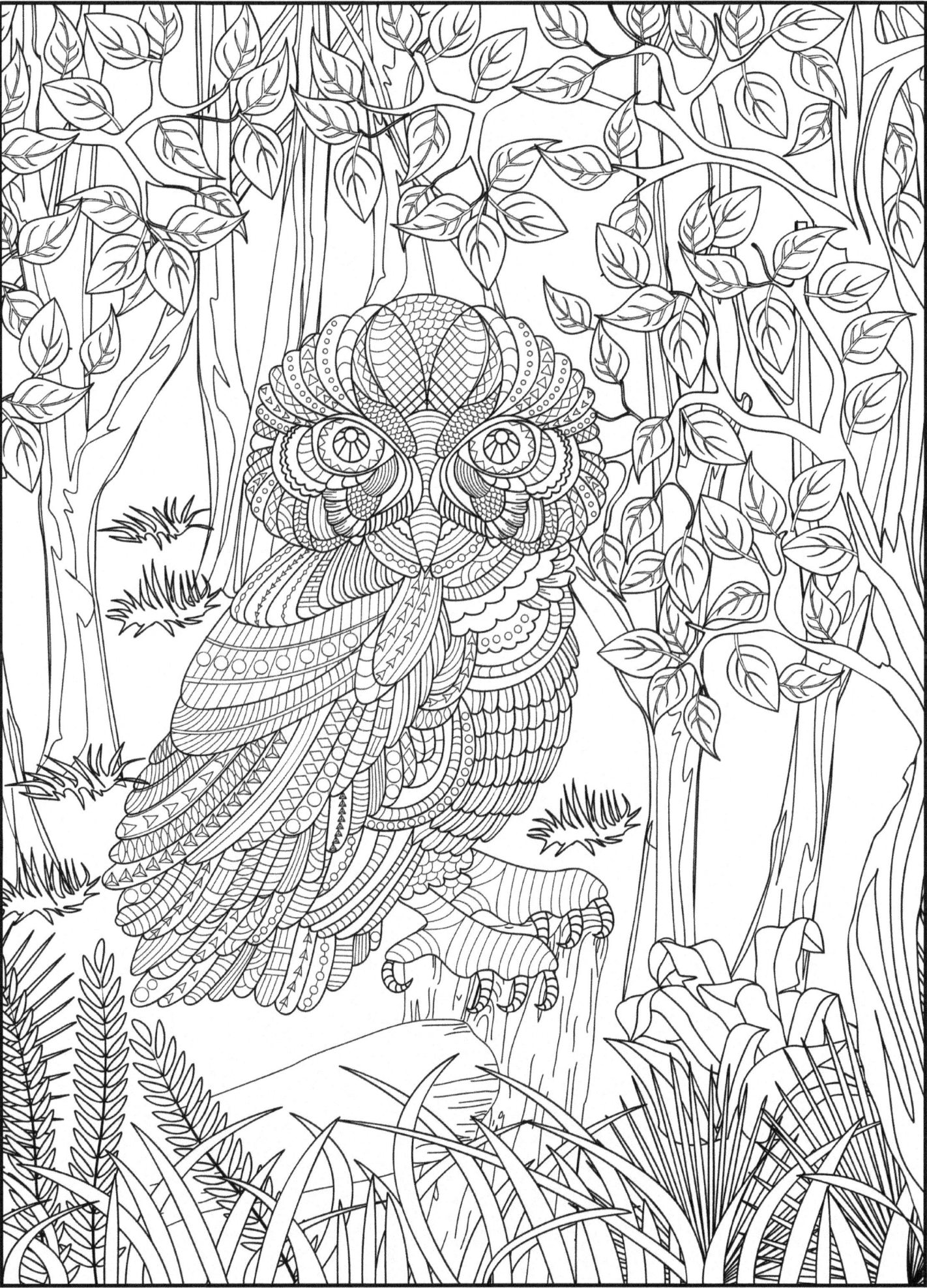

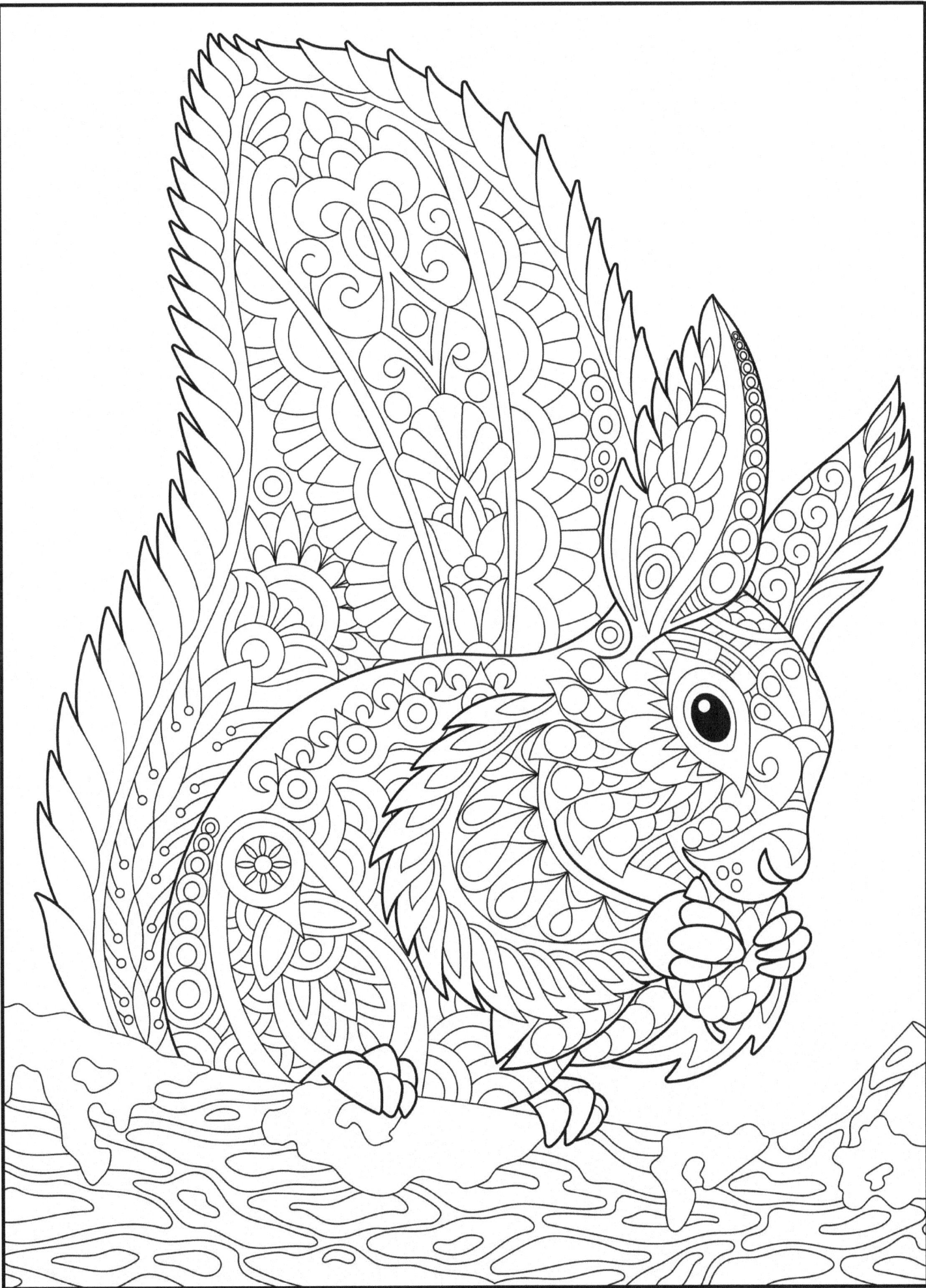

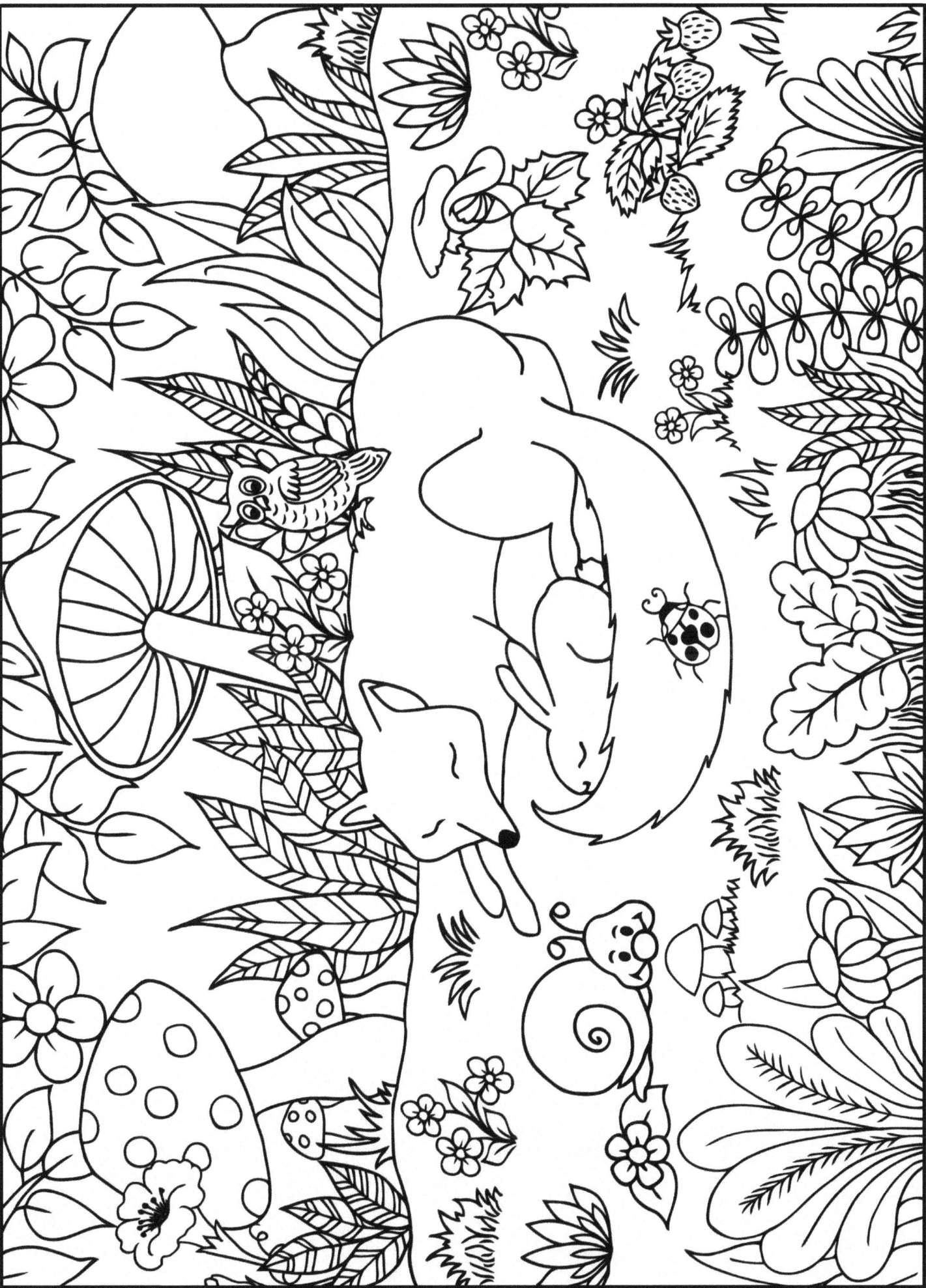

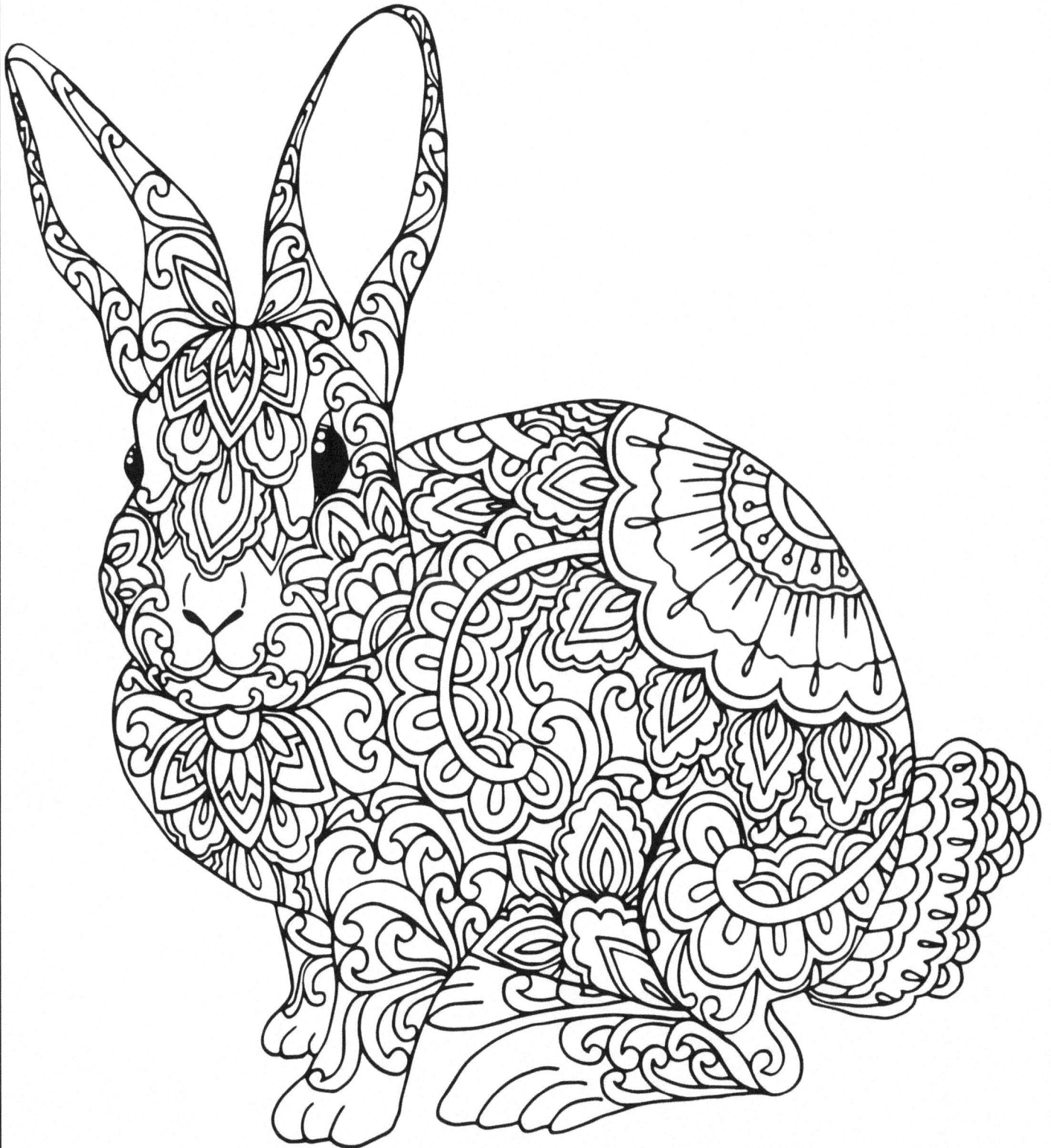

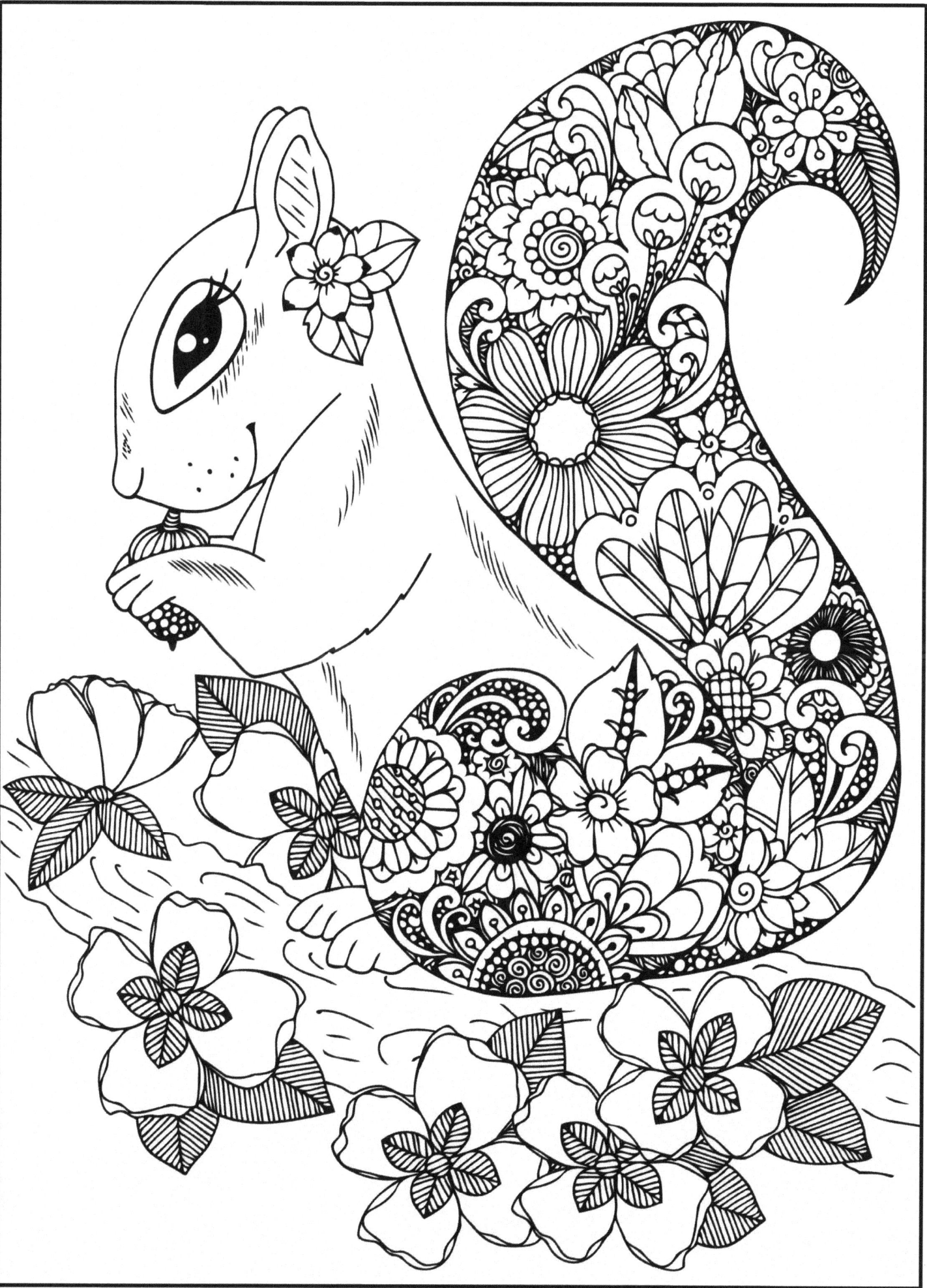

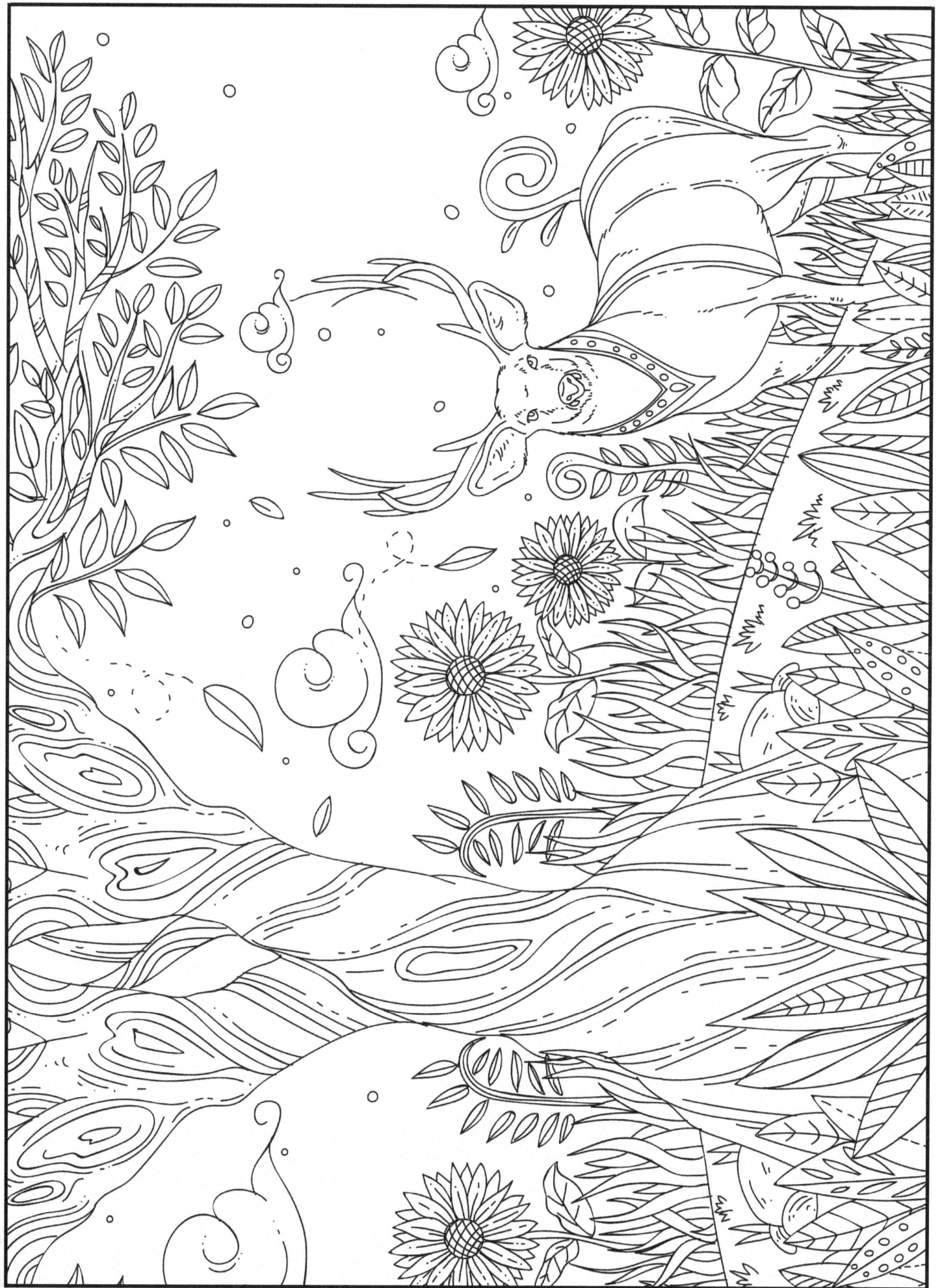

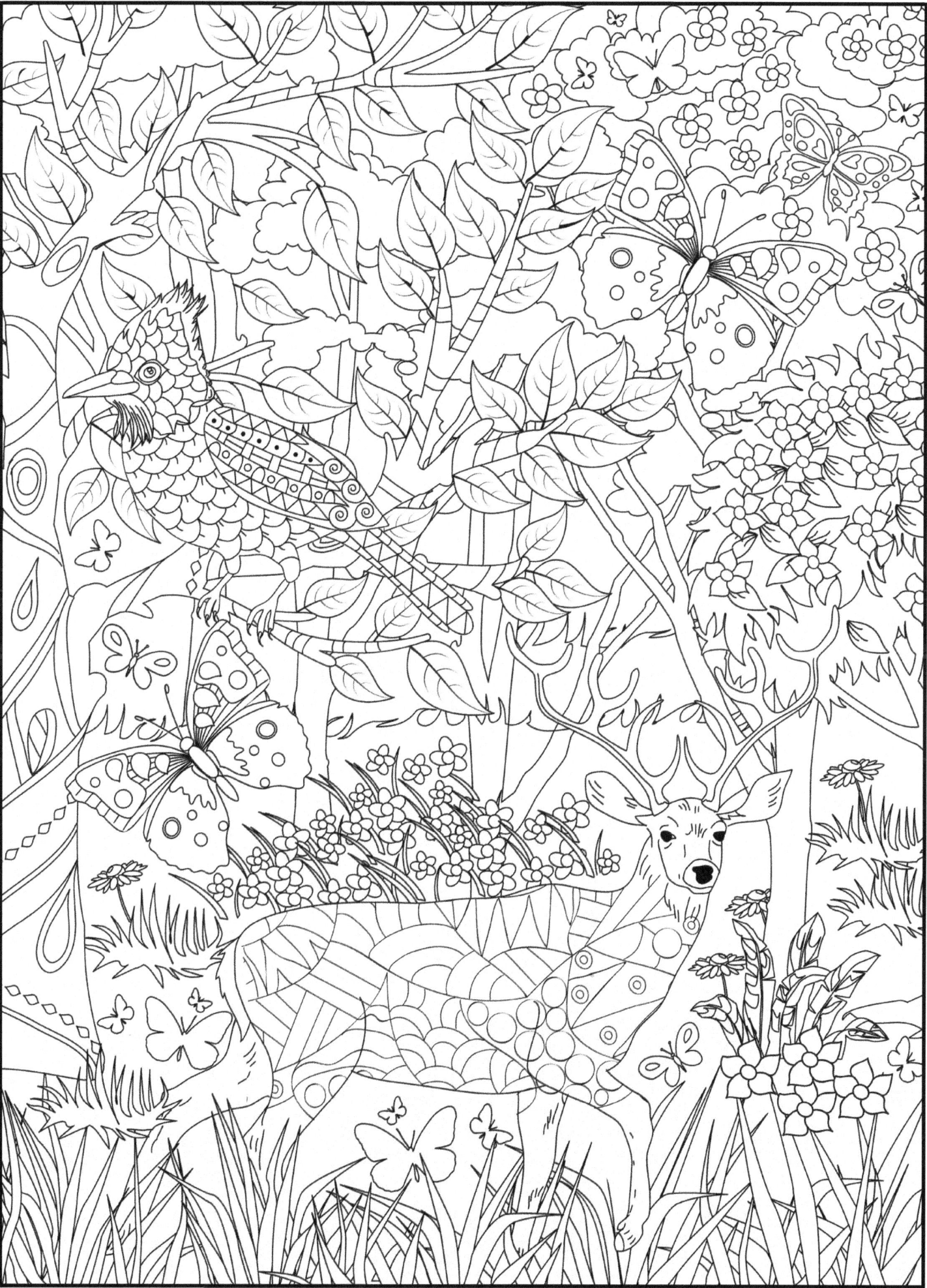

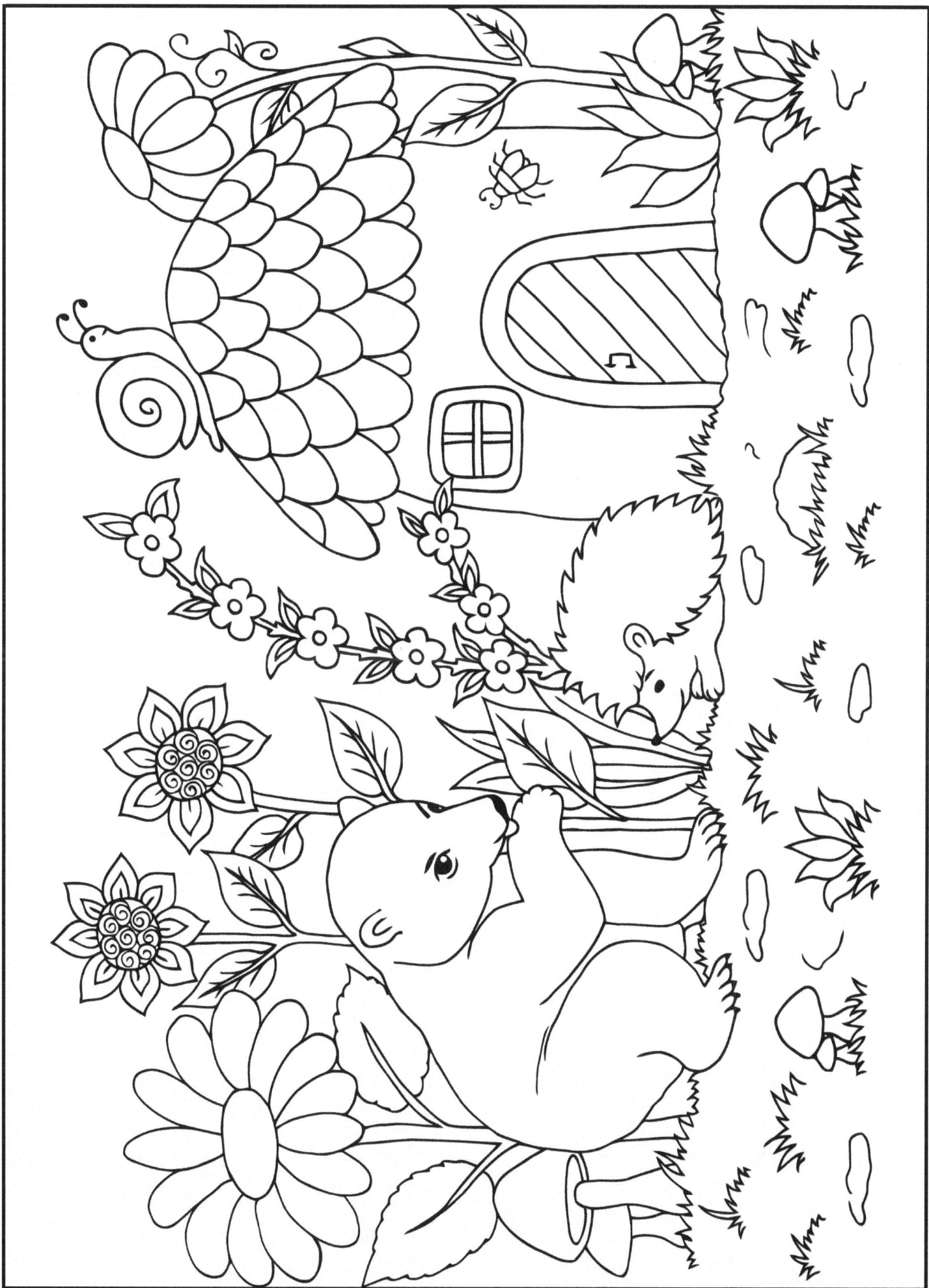

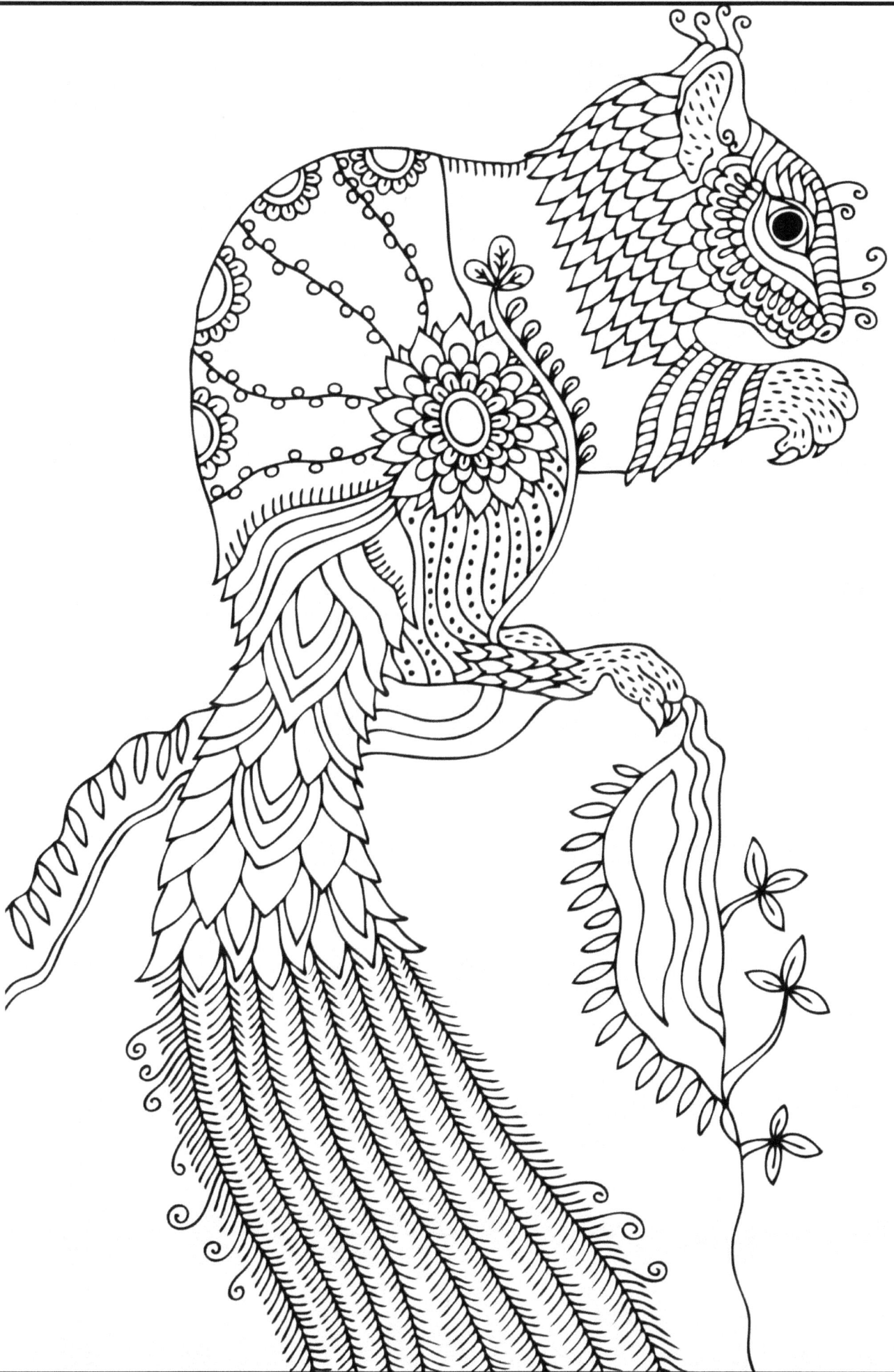

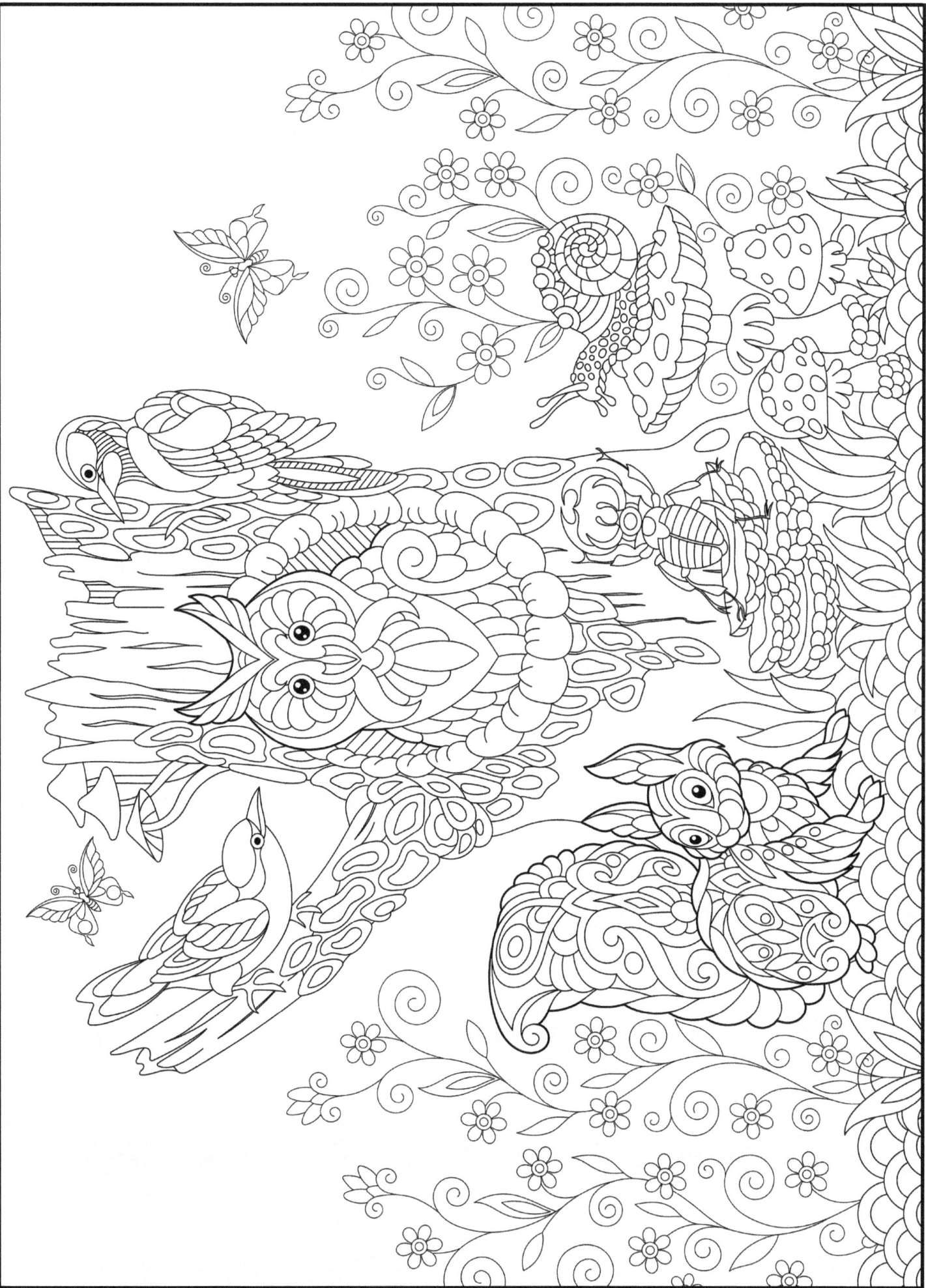

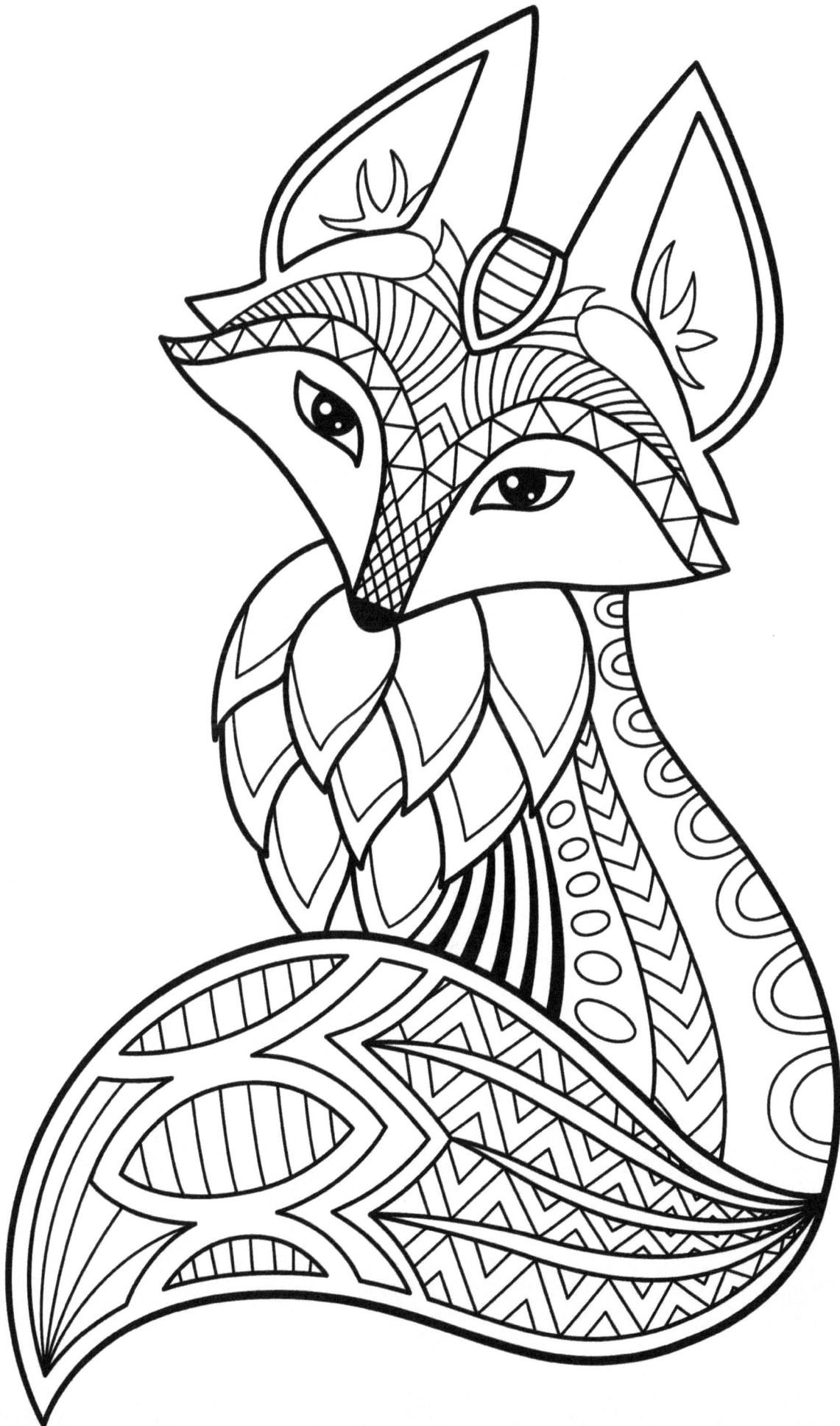

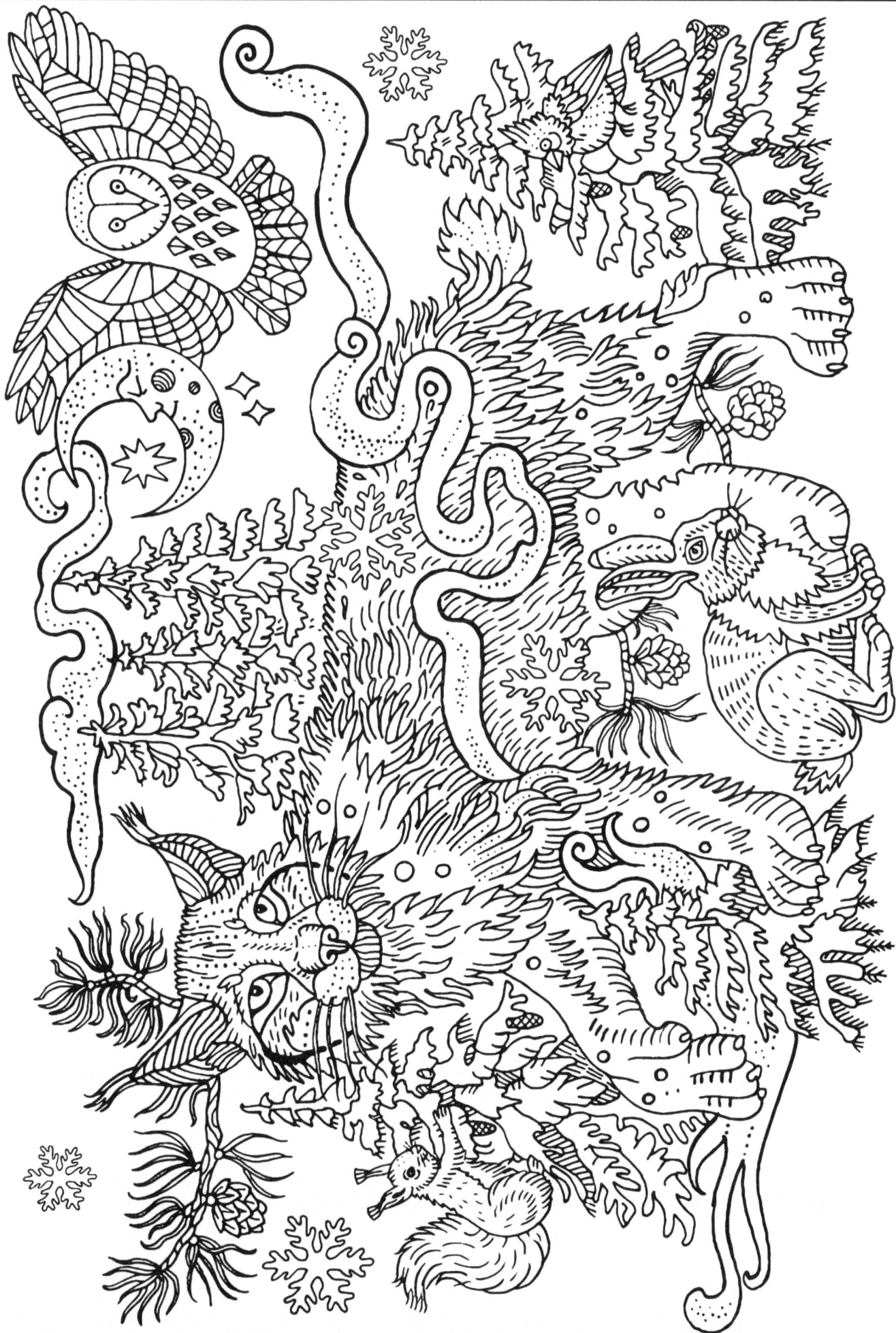

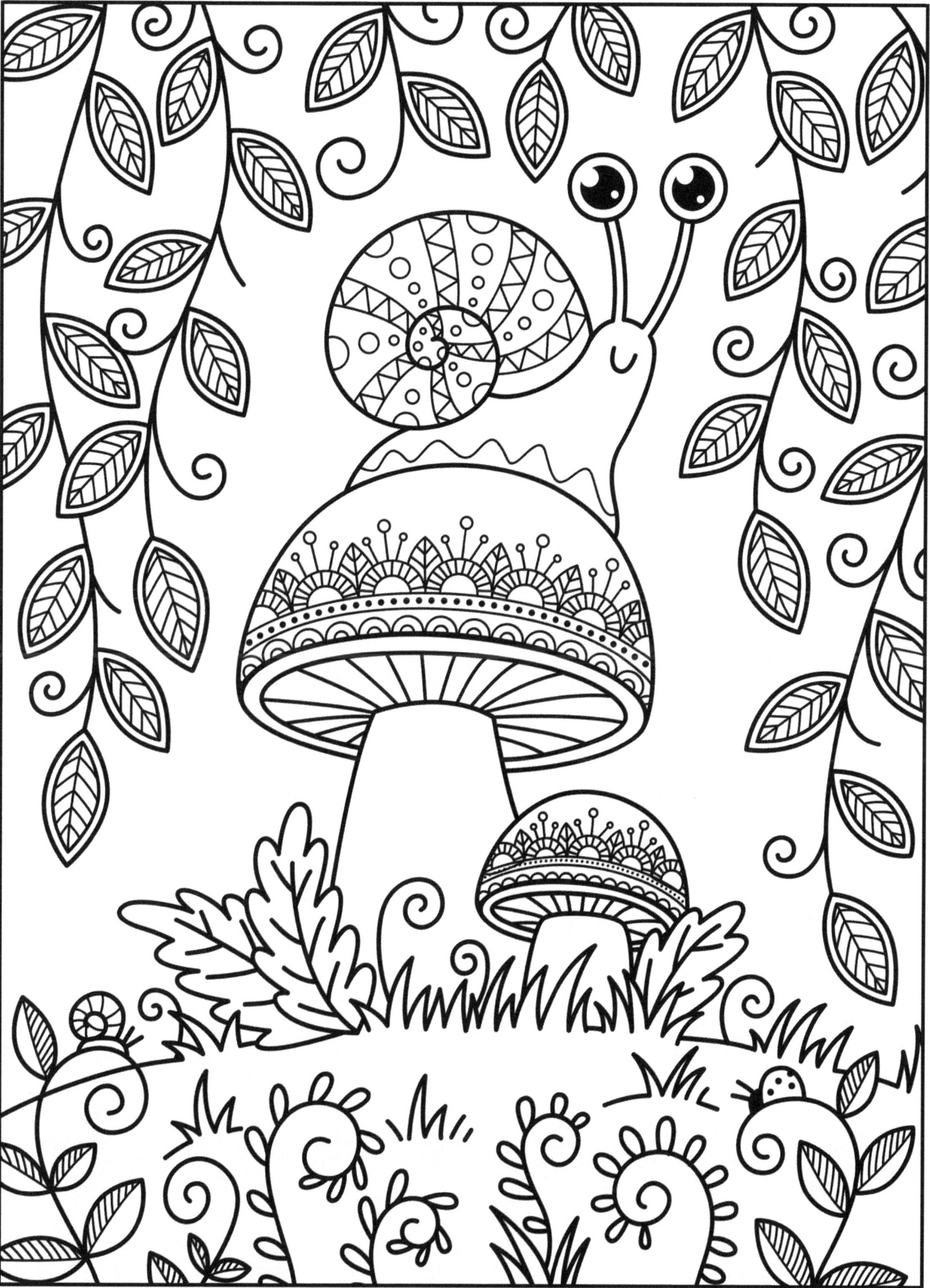

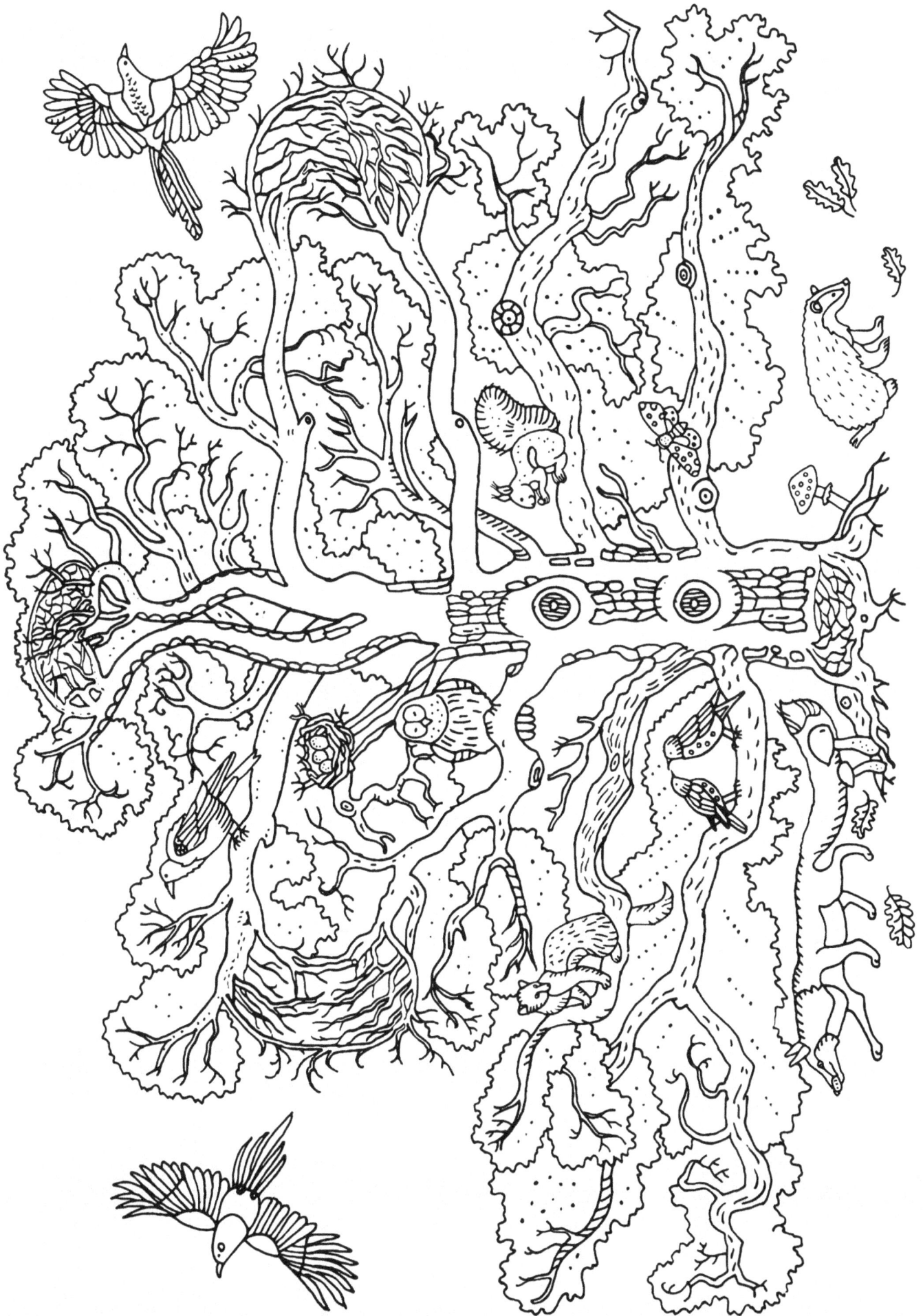

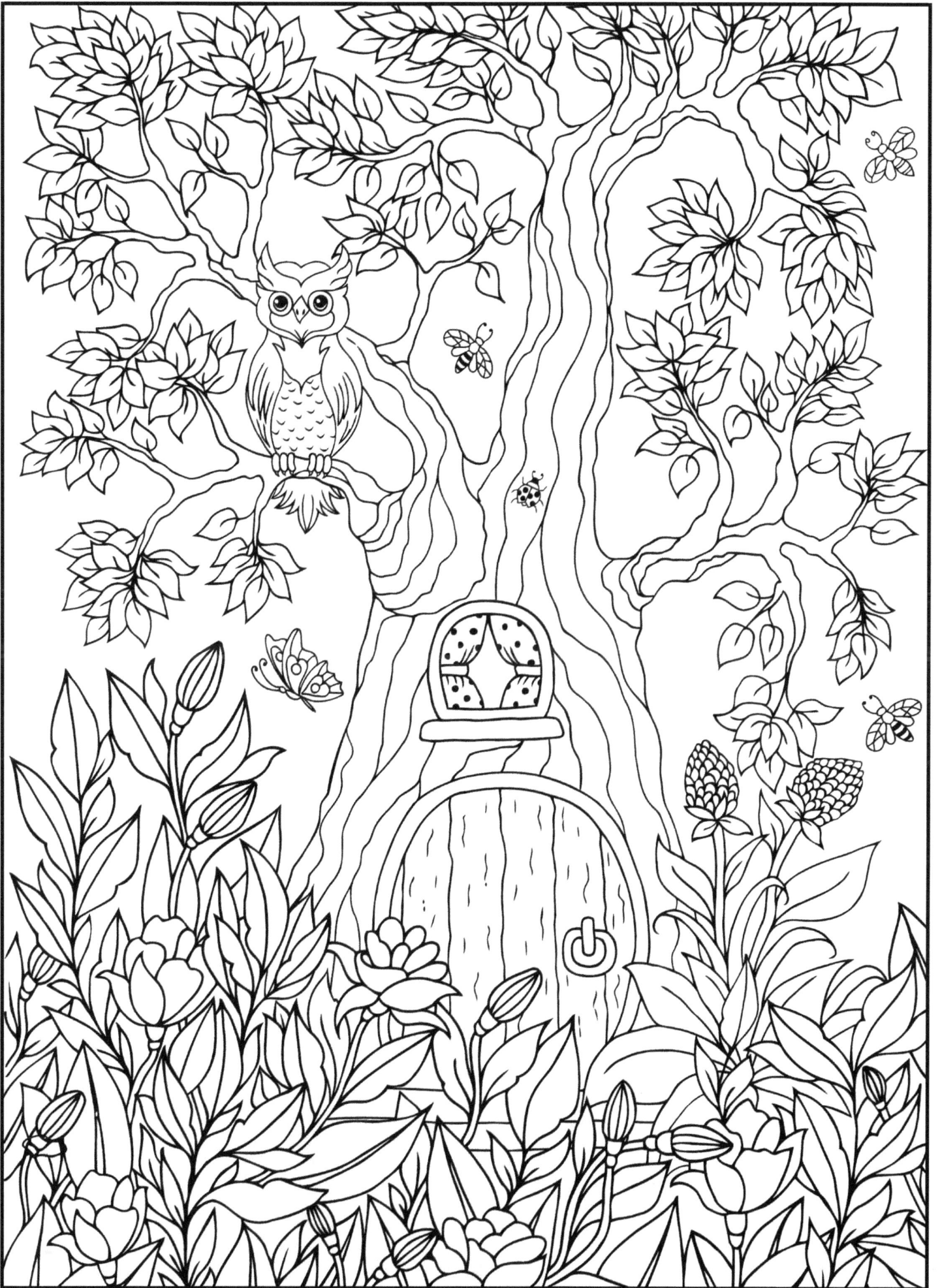

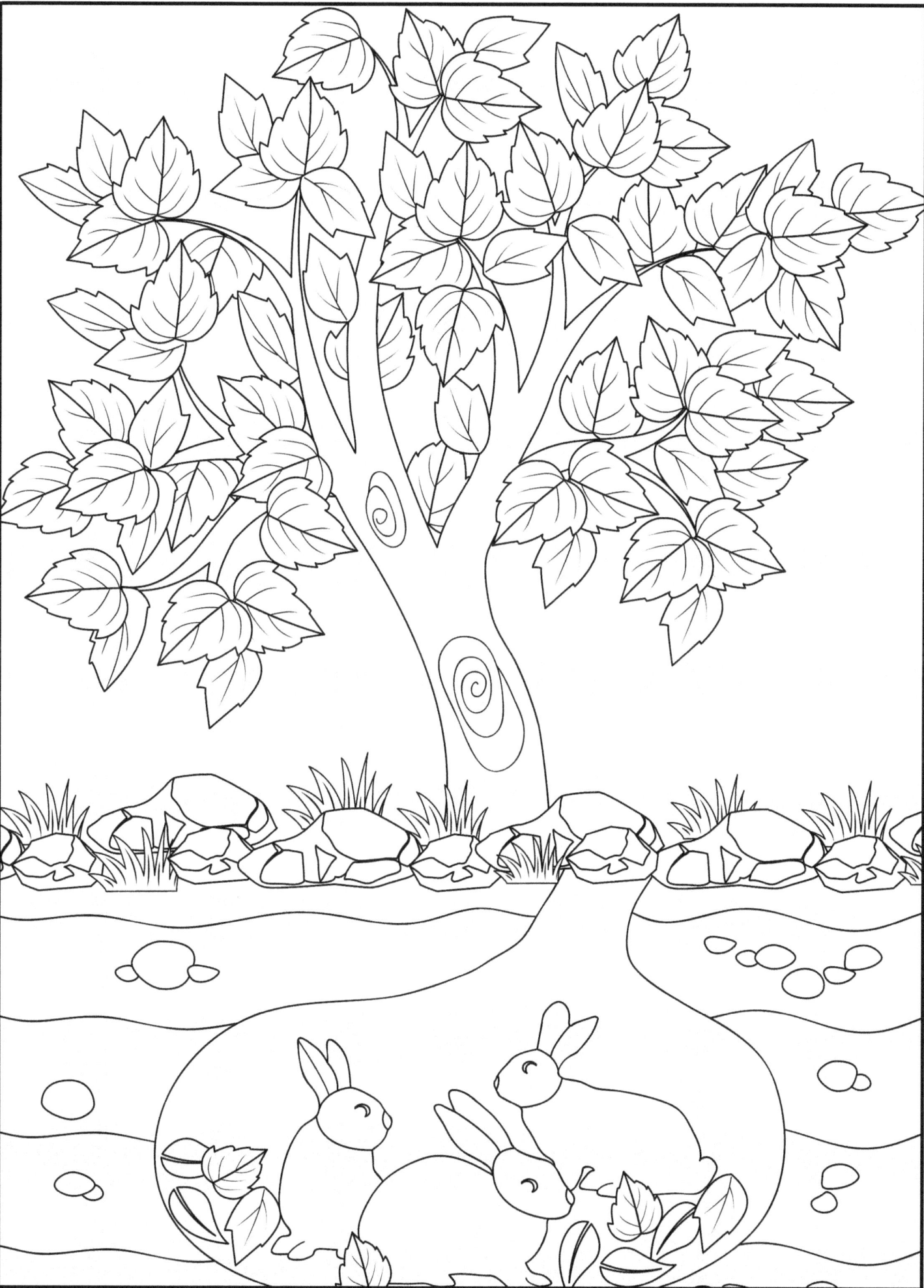

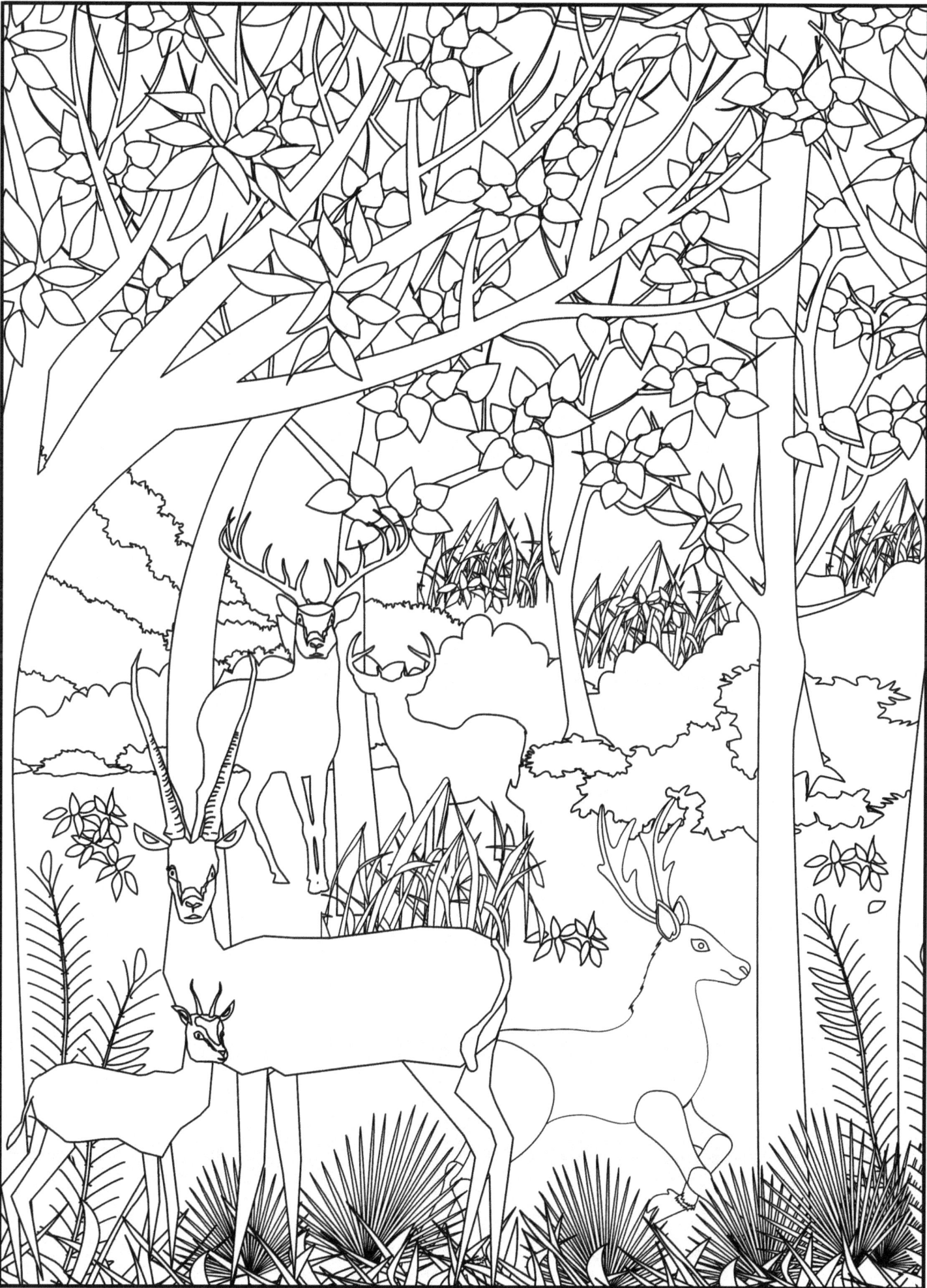

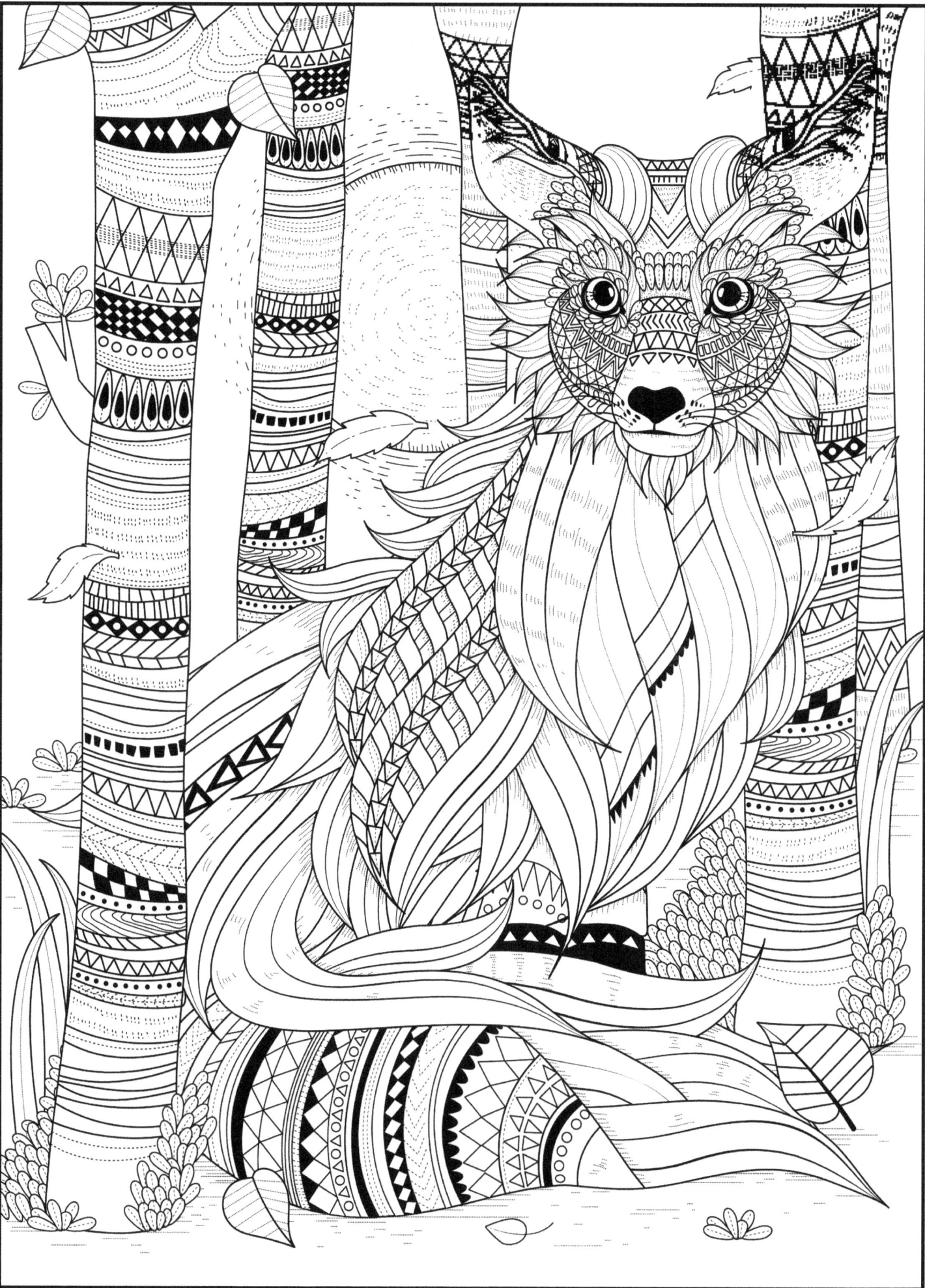

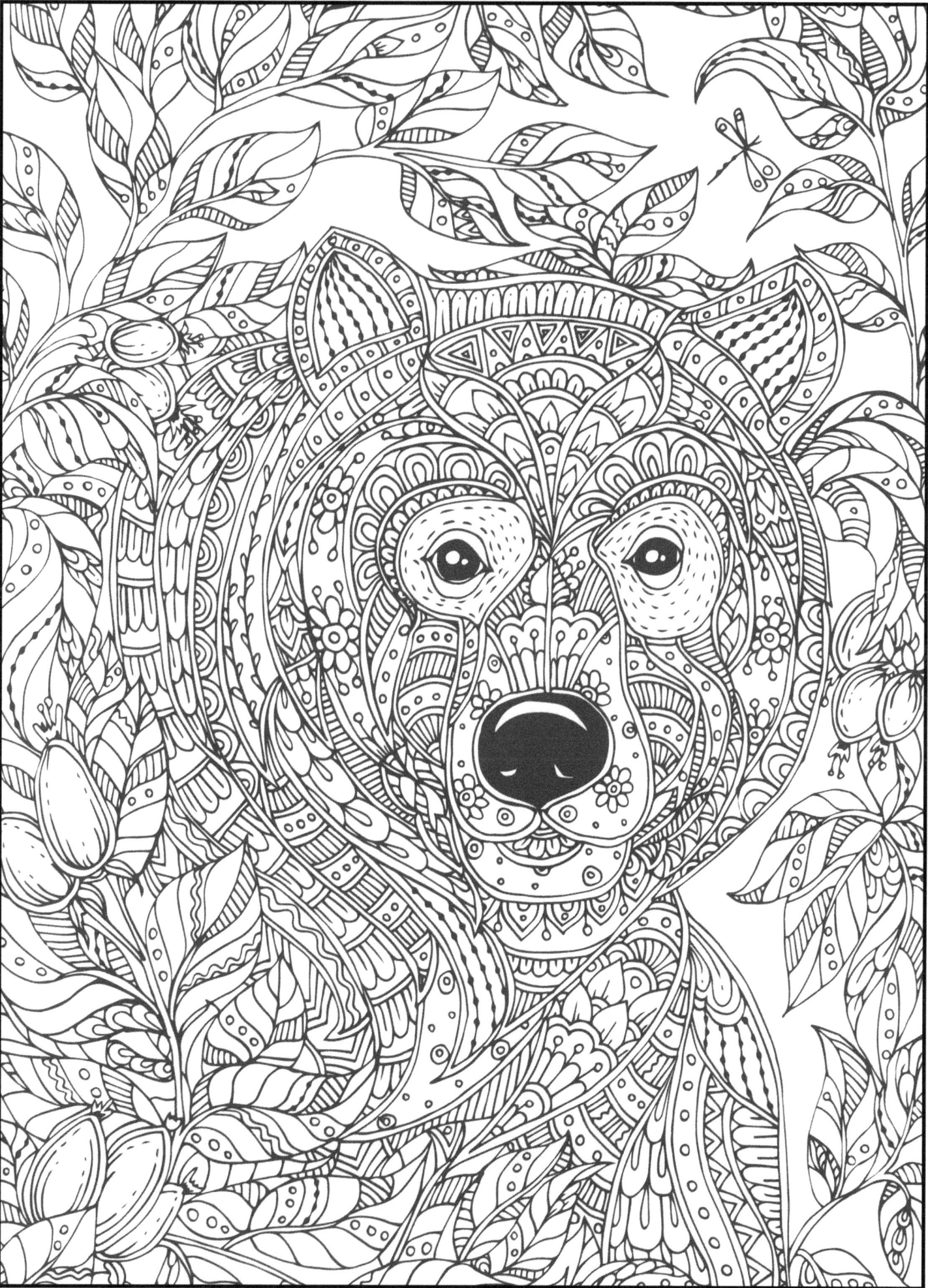

www.ingramcontent.com/pod-product-compliance
Lightning Source LLC
Chambersburg PA
CBHW080602030426
42336CB00019B/3299